WHAT HAPPENS NEXT
CHANGES EVERYTHING

WHAT HAPPENS NEXT
CHANGES EVERYTHING

Harley Hanson

INTRODUCTION

What Happens Next Changes Everything by Harley Hanson

This book will take you on a journey to give you a unique understanding of what you are and what you are truly capable of by unlocking an amazing power that lies within you!

The following chapters are laid out as a step-by-step guide of information, giving you a unique and greater understanding of the world around you.

It will teach you how everything in life is connected, and when we become aware of this magnificent power, we can use it to our advantage.

Soon you will understand the great power of the subconscious mind and its effects on your daily life. When you become aware of the mind's inner workings and the principles in this book, you can take control of your life like never before, and open new doors to your future.

You will go on a journey with the author, learning about some of the ancient and forgotten teachings on the power of the mind.

We will also look at modern-day science and its advancements in research on quantum mechanics—this book will show you that the teachings and words of lost wisdom from thousands of years ago were 100 percent correct. Once you become aware of this information, everything changes—if you choose to accept it.

Do you want the motivation to change your life?

Do you want to understand how you can change your life and even your reality?

Are you willing and dedicated to using your time to gain an understanding of how you can better your life's achievements and goals?

Maybe it's your financial status, your love life, or even your health situation—whatever it is, you would like to improve. You will find many answers to your questions in this book.

The author's intention and personal belief is that this book holds the keys and knowledge to help you turn things around in your own life from here on.

It will give you a better state of mind and a strong belief in your own control and hidden power.

Never again to accept failure or life's circumstances as if they were set in stone.

Your new positive mind-set will rewrite old habits pushing you forward to achieving greater things making the impossible possible.

(Everything is energy, whether you realize it or not!)
ARE YOU READY TO UNLOCK YOUR FULL POTENTIAL?

AUTHOR'S INTRODUCTION BY HARLEY HANSON

If I told right now that you, and only you, create your reality, I think you would find it hard to digest this philosophy. However, when you understand and use the information in this book correctly you will soon come to realize, both consciously and unconsciously, that inside you lies a great force of power and you and only you have the capability to use it and, when used correctly, it will change your life.

I personally believe there is no limit to what we are capable of; the possibilities are endless. Throughout our history, we can find amazing achievements that have been accomplished through the power of the mind.

Amazing thinkers used the power of their imagination to reshape the course of human history.

There is no limit to the potential of your power as long as you understand the universal laws that have been there since the dawn of human time. you can read more about this later.)

Some of you may think at this point that this is some kind of mumbo jumbo or crazy talk. Some of you may even think I have lost mind.

But let me reassure you that I am completely sane—well, I hope so—I don't have anything on paper that states otherwise.

I am pretty sure by the time you have finished reading this book you will come to realize that this is not some mumbo jumbo. It is simply a guide of valuable information to help you and to encourage you to change everything you want to change.

Soon it will all become clear; you will become aware of your emotions and how they produce both the cause and the effect that they have on your daily life.

You will learn how to control how you feel and act from here on out.

You will soon understand that your thoughts are vibrations, and your vibration affects the world around you. Whatever you think you are, you are.

You will understand how to create your own reality, and how to attract the opportunities and the future you been wishing for wanting and hoping for.

You will look at life through a new set of eyes. You will open doors that you thought could never be opened to you.

Motivation. Energy. Power. Money. Knowledge. Yes, it's all possible as long as you believe. As the old saying goes:

IF YOU BELIEVE, YOU ACHIEVE.

As I write this, I'm thinking of you, the reader, reading this for the first time.

For me, in the present, it's like a time machine of information—my gift to you. As I sit here writing, I'm thinking about how I'm going to formulate each word for you so that nothing is lost and the information will be presented clearly and correctly, and hopefully without spelling mistakes. It's amazing, because if you're reading this then I have accomplished my goal, and I sincerely believe it will change lives for the better.

The information on the pages following is what some might say is a philosophy of self-help. You could say it is a greater understanding of what we really are and, at the same time, an uncovering of ancient wisdom passed down from generations then connected to modern-day scientific research. Well, it's all of the above. If you are already aware of the subject matter in this book, it could be that you believe that my findings on the subject are one of life's biggest secrets—either way, I'm presenting it to you the best way I can.

I will do my best to make the reading experience as interesting and insightful as possible.

Before we start, please let me state for the record that I do not consider myself a writer or a teacher of any kind.

However, the information, as I have come to understand, is of great value to any thinking soul that wishes to change their life for the better.

I do strongly believe that this knowledge can be a great resource to you who is reading this. My hope is to give you a greater understanding of yourself and your inner workings.

I am giving you the key to change your life, and your reality from inside out.

Simply put, to change EVERYTHING...

So here I am, writing my first book. In the beginning, it was an idea. However, by the time I put the pen to the paper, it became a desire, and that one desire became a burning desire.

My first desire was to write this book to pass something down to my children. I knew in my heart that this information/knowledge would be of great benefit to them. When I look back on my own life, I feel I have wasted so many years of my life, and what I have now come to understand would hopefully save them from doing the same. It would open their eyes to the world around them, giving them a greater understanding of what is truly possible, and the potential power of the human mind. It is a simple mind-set and self-belief that would alter their current course in life. They would come to see that anything that the mind can conceive and truly believe will be manifested into their lives.

I thought this would be the ultimate gift from a parent's point of view, using what I have researched and learned to give them a head start in life and a positive mind-set.

I love my children very much, just as any loving parent does. All we want is our children's happiness and to start them on the right path in life.

Whatever the mind conceives and believes, it can achieve.—Napoleon Hill

As I see in my daily life, so many people struggling, so many people going through life with no major plan or goal, they seem to get stuck in the same old routine with little or no understanding of how to change it.

To put it more simply, they conform, they go through life on a kind of autopilot, accepting their lot and their misfortunes as if it is all out of their control.

Many people have a belief that their financial status is out of their control. They live only in hope for better days, hoping their luck will change, praying for that one lucky break.

There are also those people who are controlled and stuck in their own negative emotions due to their beliefs or past experiences, never to question what could be. (If only they knew!)

Now I have come to realize how so many people would benefit from this information—not only my children but also others out there searching for a chance of understanding how to change their lives. So, I decided to step up my motive, and that is why this book is available to you now.

I truly believe that this knowledge will change everything, and I sincerely wish somebody had introduced me to this Twenty years ago, but I also now know that it is never too late. It does not matter whether you are 18 or 65, we all have the power to change our lives for the better. We all have the power to have and to do what we once called our dreams. (Yes, I said WHAT WE ONCE CALLED OUR DREAMS, because soon you will learn that anything is possible.)

By picking up this book, you have taken the first step. Maybe it's your curiosity, or maybe it's no coincidence that you are reading this. There is a reason for everything. I would like you, the reader, to go through this book with an open mind, because for some of you this information can go against your understanding of life so far.

It can also contradict some of your core beliefs.

Please be patient.

Since the day you were born, you have been programmed by observation. Everything you have experienced and been taught is what has built up your current belief system. Your life's experiences so far have molded your mind just like a computer program—once in place, it becomes hardwired and anything that goes against this program is deleted or not accepted. It is the same with your belief system—any new information that we do not believe will simply be dismissed. That is why I said it can go against your core beliefs, because sometimes new information cannot be accepted. So please have an open mind, I'm sure you will benefit from this later.

Through a little patience and commitment to reading this book, you will soon understand my goal, which is to help you change your life and get to where you want to be. By learning this simple but wide spectrum of knowledge, you can unlock the keys to a happier and more successful life.

Remember, you have nothing to lose but everything to gain.

The magic and the secret of this information, as I have come to understand it, is that it has been around for centuries. There are those who believe that this information has only been available to a select few groups or certain individuals of power. Like all information, if you know where to look, and connect the dots, you can find it. I don't think it's necessary to write about the conspiracy theories on this subject, as that will only change your focus and fill your mind with unnecessary information. But I can assure you, there have been many writers and philosophers writing on the matter. You can choose yourself whether you want to go down that road, but right here and now it is important to focus on what will help you.

So, let us go on this journey together; stay with me.

When I first stumbled upon this knowledge, I was in shock. It was like my whole life flashed before me—pieces of information that I had learned or heard about over my years started connecting together. It was a little bit like the feeling we call, *deja vu*. I had a million questions about life, and not a single answer. The big WHY—why are some people rich and others poor. Why are some people happy and others sad? Why some people have amazingly good luck and others have none.

I had a strong feeling when I began this journey that the answers, I was looking for would come to my attention and, oh boy, did they! It was like I was being guided by some unseen force. My curiosity got the better of me, and so it began. With a strong impulse, I started reading and researching everything I could get my hands on, from quantum mechanics to the law of attraction teachings. But that was not enough; I needed to understand where it all came from.

I started to search the origins of all great teachings and philosophies on what separates us and why some are successful and others live in constant failure. I also looked back through history at the great minds like Nikola Tesla, Thomas Edison, Albert Einstein. They all seemed to have a greater understanding of the powers of the universe. Philosophers like Socrates and Plato all had a great unique understanding on the subject, and it was mind-blowing how it all connected. It was like the knowledge and understanding had been right in front of us all the time. In many modern-day religions or religious teachings, you see the same teachings over and over again, making us aware of the power within—however, it all seems to be lost in translation. It doesn't matter what faith you believe in; the principles are the same.

I just wanted to point out that this information is nothing new; it has always been there, it's just a matter of how we come to understand it.

In the Bible, you will find:

For everyone who asks receives; he who seeks finds; and to him who knocks, the door will be opened. – Matthew 7: 8.

Buddha said, "What we are today comes from our thoughts of yesterday, and our present thoughts build our life of tomorrow: Our life is the creation of our mind."

Gandhi said, "A man is but the product of his thoughts. What he thinks he becomes."

No matter how far you go back in our known history, you find the same evident information and teachings. In many ancient cultures and even in mythology, you will see it present. I just find all this fascinating.

Trying to piece together all this information was no easy task. I was very careful about what I studied, because I now know that there is a lot of misleading information out there, but every source of information can be cross-referenced, every major key of information can be traced back to an original source.

I dedicated my time to better my life, sticking to credible teachings and philosophies of success.

But most important, I put the information to the test. My life has become one big experiment.

And I now know there is a process to understanding this universal knowledge. Like any other formula, you must learn the correct process of how to implement this knowledge to your daily life...

There are many self-help books out there and many gurus and teachers promising a formula or method to change your life.

But I'm not writing this to preach to you or to promise you riches. Instead, I'm going to take you step-by-step through a sequence of learning and knowing how to apply some of the forgotten wisdom and newly discovered findings into your daily life.

Since I have discovered what you are about to learn, my life has literally turned around for the better. To this day it continues to surprise me—the amazing results that are possible when one understands and truly believes in their own magnificent power. I'm always expanding my knowledge on these subjects. It is important to keep learning because we don't know what we don't know.

So, what did I get out this information?

What gives me the right to tell you the reader about this?

I could tell you my life story and how I have come to understand where I went wrong in my earlier years through a lack of this knowledge. I could tell you how my negative emotions controlled me. How my limited view of life held me back from excelling. But this will not help you! We all have a life story, and I'm not going to bore you with that. You don't need distractions about my life. It is your life and your future that is important, so let me keep you in the main focus.

I will share with you some simple facts about my results so far.

1. My financial status has completely changed. I have accomplished what I believed earlier to be impossible.

The more I learned, the more my income, surprisingly, increased.

The house I previously thought was not possible, I now own.

The car I visioned having is now mine—it all was accomplished by this knowledge.

I'm not what you would call rich but I now have the mind-set that anything is possible; the results are there.

IT IS NOT THE HOW, IT'S SIMPLY KNOWING YOU HAVE IT ALL READY.

2. I have learned the process to control my emotions and the way I feel with a positive mind-set.

I control my thoughts and feelings, meaning my actions and views on life have a positive outlook.

I have reprogrammed my core beliefs. I recreated my personality to benefit my future.

My attitude toward life = life's attitude toward me.

3. My goals and dreams that I have set for myself have been achieved or are in the process of being accomplished.

Every time I have had a new idea, all I needed to complete it would fall into place as long as I knew how to focus and had the right attitude to succeed.

I will always continue to develop new ideas, new projects, new dreams. We have one life and everything is possible.

If you set your destination you know where you're going.—Harley Hanson

4. My understanding of life and the difference between success and failure, wealth or poverty is all in our control. This is not an understatement if we have the power to think and educate ourselves. With the correct knowledge and beliefs, anything is possible.

Change begins with fresh eyes, in other words. It begins with an awakened imagination.—Mark Buchanan

5. By developing an attractive and winning personality, I have learned how to attract people and opportunities into my life in order to help me reach my end goal and build a better future for myself and for others.

ATTITUDE = SUCCESS

These are just a few simple examples of how learning what you are about to read has changed my life for the better. There is no limit to what we can do when we know how to do it. All you have is the present moment right here right now! Yesterday is gone and tomorrow is not here yet. So, the present moment is all you have, and in the present moment you can commit to creating a better future for yourself. If you are willing and motivated, anything is possible. Are you ready? Come on, let's open Pandora's box together...

CONTENTS

CHAPTER 1

UNDERSTANDING WHAT YOU ARE

THE MIND NEEDS TIME TO process all new information. We also need time to build faith in any new knowledge that is presented to us. It is then our own individual choice to accept or dismiss it. However, if there are certain things in your life you want to change or improve, you must be willing to give a new understanding a chance.

Ask yourself what you have got to lose by reading this book. It is possible the title of this book will help you understand why you should read on.

The information in this book at times may seem like it is been repeated, or the same information has been formulated in a different context but basically means the same. There is a strong reason for this, and as you read through the chapters, all will be revealed. I hope it will be a journey of enlightenment for you.

The basic truth is, if we keep doing what we have always done we keep getting the same results. Faith and understanding go a long way when you want to achieve something and build a better future for yourself. That is also why this book has been written in a specific order to help you to understand and benefit fully from the information on the pages that follow. Just like the world's strongest structures—skyscrapers, bridges, houses, etc.—everything must be built upon a strong foundation. The same goes for the human mind. Your mind is like the foundation—the stronger the foundation, the more you can construct. If our foundation is weak, over a short time, things will simply fall apart. In the context of this book, you will be right back where you started. It is the same in all human endure and achievement—the more we understand and believe and backed by faith the greater the ability of the mind to achieve.

There is a great power that lies within us all, but first we need to absorb the knowledge and the teachings of the great potential of the human mind. I personally have come to believe that this knowledge has the power to reshape our reality to our choosing.

If we are going to truly understand and develop this great power that lies within us, we need to understand what we are working with; we need to start at the beginning of everything.

So in order to do this, we will start at the subatomic level.

So, WHAT ARE WE?

I remember back when I was at school and just for the record, I was the kid that never really paid attention in class. I was briefly told that everything on the planet is made of matter, including me, and that matter is made of tiny little atoms, and that these atoms are made up of three tiny particles that are called subatomic particles:

protons, neutrons, and electrons. I guess you already know this because you went to school and paid attention. Just in case you have forgotten, here is a quick recap.

The protons and neutrons make up the center of the atom called the nucleus, and the electrons fly around above the nucleus in something like a small cloud. When I think back, this was about the extent of my knowledge on the subject. Like most children, I never really put any thought into it or even questioned what it all really means. I took myself and my surroundings for granted.

However, that has all changed now so I'll try to do my best to explain the best way I can. I am by no means a scientist or a specialist on the subject. However, I do find it all very interesting, and the more I learn, the more my awareness develops. I hope that after each chapter you too will come to understand things the way I have. When this happens, you will become more conscious. You will become more aware of the world around you and what makes you who you are.

I will use some scientific findings and research from some brilliant minds that have dedicated their lives to understanding what we are and how everything is connected. The new findings are changing the world of science, and more and more people are waking up to this information. This is the first stage of the book. It is also a key principle and the beginning of your foundation.

From a young age, I have always been curious about life and the differences in quality of life. Tried to work out why some people had everything while others had nothing, why some people had great achievements and others remained dormant with no real purpose in life. I think if I'm completely honest, in my younger years I always wondered what it would take to build an amazing life myself, what would be necessary to go from nothing to fulfill my desires and dreams. My curious mind has taken me on many endeavors in search of these answers, I could always find motivation but I lacked knowledge. The first step happened when I stumbled upon the subject of Quantum Mechanics.

For those of you who do not know what Quantum Mechanics is, it is the theory that explains the amazing nature and behavior of matter/atoms on a subatomic level.

Don't ask me why or how I became interested in this subject, because I can't answer you. It is like something just got a hold of me and pulled me in. The more I learned, the more I wanted to know. This was the starting point of my journey for knowledge. I now believe that this is the foundation. I mentioned earlier this will all tie into everything else you learn later on.

Don't worry, I'm not going to blast you with loads of science theories, but as you read through this book you will see that this information is of great importance. It will help you to see and understand the amazing possibility that is in front of you in self-development, and give you life-changing results from here on. Simply put, to Change Everything.

YOU KNOW WHAT YOU KNOW, BUT YOU DON'T KNOW WHAT YOU DON'T KNOW.

Part 1: What You Are on Quantum Level

A Disclaimer—Everyone has a theory or a limited view. You can believe whatever you want, but you don't get to misinterpret scientific findings.

When it comes to who or what we are and our great potential as the human species, the information presented to you in this book may make you question what you already know. But my hope is, sooner or later you will understand that the power inside of you is just waiting to be used, and it will benefit your future. The findings and discoveries are out there, and scientists continue to make great leaps in these discoveries with some fascinating and interesting results that are relevant to this book.

When we took a science class in basic school, all the scientific information we learned is becoming or seems to be outdated because the scientific community is always making new advancements.

Throughout our known history, there have been some great scientists and theorists. One of the most well-known scientists and mathematicians from England was Isaac Newton (1642–1726). His theories and equations are well-known, like the theory of gravity, which is known today as Newton's law of gravity.

It is something we all know and it is taught to our children even today. Newton's theories and research, along with his name, have gone down in the history books. However, since Newton's days, the scientific community and technology have rapidly advanced, especially in the last century. It is strangely clear that Newton's science theories were not applicable to extremely small particles. A new type of science was born—this science was called Quantum physics or quantum mechanics—call it what you will, the interesting findings are the same and what they have discovered is mind-bending. Yet it also teaches us a great principle of what we are and how the universe works. Not only that, but it also shows us the potential power of the human mind.

There have been some great minds working in the field of Quantum Physics: Niels Bohr, Eugene Wigner, Werner Heisenberg, Max Born, Thomas Young.

Niels Bohr (1885–1962) was one of the fathers of Quantum Physics. You could say his theories on atomic structures helped shape the way we look and research the world today. These minds put in motion a new way for us to look at the universe and how everything works in harmony, making the scientific world now question reality.

Quantum physics/Quantum Mechanics has shown again and again that there is no such thing as solid matter. It simply does not exist in the known universe. Everything in the universe is made of atoms—that we know—but with the advancements in scientific equipment and understanding, they have found that atoms are not solid. As mankind has developed the technology to look deeper into the atom structure, what we see is the three different sub-atomic particles as you would expect to find—protons, neutrons, and electrons. But when they look even deeper into the atom structure, they see nothing but an empty void. Everything is held together by invisible forces or vibrations. The atom itself has no physical structure.

So, think about it for a moment. Process this information. It's like Alice in Wonderland going down the rabbit hole, at least it was for me when I started to study this information. It was like a big light came on in my head—so many questions, and I become hungry for the knowledge. Everything in our reality is made up of atoms, but nothing that we see, including ourselves, has a solid physical structure, because all atoms are made and comprised of invisible energy, and we now know that this energy is constantly vibrating.

As documented time and time again, atoms are actually made up of 99.99999 percent ENERGY/SPACE/VIBRATION—call it what you will, the definition is the same. Everything, simply put, is a vibration of unseen energy. The energy that makes you and me is the same energy that makes the trees, rocks, the car you drive, the building you are in, and the chair or the bed you are using to read this book. It's all made of the same stuff—energy.

Think about this—the mountains, the buildings, they all look and feel solid but in actual fact they are vibrating at very high speeds of frequency, vibration so fast that they look and feel the way they do. Bruce Lipton has a great way for us to visualize and understand this information—he said, and I quote, "Imagine the atom as tornado swirling around at great speed. Then drive your car at 150km straight at the tornado will the car go through the tornado?" The answer is, no, it would be like hitting a stone wall. The car would be smashed to pieces. Why? Because all atoms are like miniature tornadoes. They create waves, and all of these waves put together are called a field, it's like a kind of force field.

What quantum physics teaches us is that everything we thought was physical is not physical.—Bruce H. Lipton.

Now here is another interesting fact, which relates to our life. Each atom has its own distinct frequency or vibration. Everything in the universe is vibrating all the time...

Einstein got it before we did. Here is a small quote from *Personal Development with Success.*

(Albert Einstein turned the scientific world on edge in 1905 with his simple but powerful equation, E=mc2. In this equation, Einstein told the scientific community what possibility thinkers in the philosophical community already knew—that everything is made of energy.)

The study of quantum physics has proven beyond doubt that the physical world that we know of is just one large sea of energy. Nothing is solid; everything is made up of nonphysical stuff, energy. I can't say the word energy enough—it is one of the main factors you need to understand and accept. You and everything around you is a vibration of energy. When you understand this, you are ready to move forward.

If quantum mechanics hasn't profoundly shocked you, you haven't understood it yet. Everything we call real is made of things that cannot be regarded as real.—Niels Bohr

One of the most famous experiments in the Quantum world was the double-slit experiment done by physicist Thomas Young back in

1801. What it demonstrated was unexpected. It showed that little particles of matter had something of a wave about them. It also showed that when being observed, this had a dramatic effect on the behavior of the particles. In the slit experiment, Young shined a light through two slits and observed interference patterns on a screen behind the slits. He found that the act of observing the particles caused changes in their behavior! In short, the particles behave differently when they are being observed by the thinking mind (*The Observer*).

It is said that it was this experiment that started science down the mind-blowing road of Quantum mechanics.

Think about it for a moment—if a particle changes its behavior when it's being observed, what do you think influences the particle?

The answer is you—the consciousness of the mind of the observer. Simply by focusing on the particle, you affect its behavior. Now think about this—everything in your world is made of the same stuff—energy. And by observing it, we can change the outcome. Einstein also suggests that time and space are dependent on the individual.

He showed that time and space are "relative," and explained how they can be viewed differently by each of us. We are the cause and the effect at the same time.

I highly recommend you watch the movie *What the Bleep! Down the Rabbit Hole—Quantum Edition*. This will explain in more detail the modern understandings on the subject. I just wanted to touch upon it briefly to help you grasp what follows. I hope your foundations are starting to form.

Everything is energy and we all have the power to change that energy.—Harley Hanson

PART 2: YOU ARE A TRANSMITTER AND RECEIVER OF FREQUENCY

We are made of atoms, and atoms are made of vibration. This means we are vibrational beings. We emit our own unique vibrational frequency. The brain is a transmitter and receiver of frequency. Your body and your mind are like a radio tower sending out and receiving signals (vibrations) all the time. Some of the greatest minds in history, like Thomas Edison, Nikola Tesla, and Albert Einstein said it best with their inspiring quotes.

The human brain emits frequency which when focused, picked up by another human brain, and does affect physical matter. It passes through the ether, through solid objects, and travels faster than the speed of light.—Thomas Edison

If you want to know the secrets of the universe, think in terms of energy, frequency, and vibration.—Nikola Tesla

Your imagination is your preview of life's coming attractions.—Albert Einstein

Albert Einstein, Thomas Edison, and Nikola Tesla, they all agreed on one thing—that every cell in the human body emits a different frequency. They also agreed that everything on planet Earth and the universe is made up of vibrational energy. This means that everything on Earth emits a frequency (a vibration) that is quantifiable and measurable. When we truly understand this, it starts to change everything we thought we knew. It will start to open the doors to your hidden power.

So here you are, a human being who has this powerful instrument for receiving and transmitting vibrations of energy. What does this really mean for us? How can we use this knowledge to change our lives for the better?

Look at it this way—on a grander scale, this means that everything in the universe is connected. Everything is made up of the same stuff; you could say it is just one big infinite field of energy, and everything, including you, is connected.

As science is continuously developing, we are finding out that our minds and feelings also have the power to affect our reality. We also see this in the animal kingdom. It is said that animals rely mostly on their senses. They can pick up the vibrations of other species and sense danger.

Have you ever walked into a room and just sensed that something or someone is negative? Have you ever thought about someone and then all of sudden they call you on the phone? Well, it's not your mind playing tricks on you. In many situations in our lives we have felt something strange. Some say it is sixth sense, but science is showing us that it is a lot more than that. We are sending and receiving vibrations of frequency all the time, and our minds pick up on those vibrations of frequency.

There are many articles and books on this subject, and years of research and experiments done by the governments of the world. Mind control, hypnosis, psychic abilities, the list goes on, but if we dig too deep, we move away from science and fall into conspiracy theories. I needed something that I could do myself to prove the effects of our thoughts on matter, so I went hunting for information I could use myself.

One of the many interesting experiments I found on my journey to prove the effects of the mind was the famous rice experiment. This is something you can try at home. If you have any doubts on this information presented to you, I suggest you try it.

The rice experiment was invented back in 2004 by an "alternative-science" researcher Masaru Emoto, who strongly believes in the literal power of thought. He was also in the movie *What the Bleep Do We Know*, the one I recommended earlier. He set out to prove that our thoughts can affect matter. The original YouTube video of Emoto performing the experiment had more than two million views and, 10 years later, many others have reproduced his experiment, with the same outstanding results. If you watch the video or one of the many others out there, you will see that Dr. Emoto places equal amounts of rice and water in three glass jars.

Each day, for thirty days, he talks to the jars of rice—to the first one, he says, "Thank you," and positive words, with emotions of love. To the second, he shouts "You idiot," sending negative emotions. To the third jar he says nothing at all, ignoring it completely, giving it no emotional signal. The results after three weeks were amazing, you could say.

The rice inside the jar to which he said "Thank you," sending positive vibrations, developed a pink color but pretty much looked the same, with no odor or decay. The rice inside the second, the jar to which he shouted, "You idiot," sending negative vibrations, was dark, and mold was growing on it, with a very bad smelling odor. The third jar that he ignored smelled bad but stayed white, with less deterioration than the second jar. These three jars proved his theory.

The rice that got the positive vibrations from the human mind stayed pretty much the same, whereas the other two jars that received negative or no vibrations rotted away.

So, think about that on a grander scale. Our thoughts and vibrations affect our reality. Masaru Emoto conducted many of these fascinating experiments that tend to prove that not just our actions but even our thoughts affect our environments. He also froze water samples that he took from around the world, and then he took pictures of the water crystal structure under the microscope. What he found was, depending on the quality of the water, you would see amazing differences in the water crystal structure. He also introduced the water samples to different kinds of vibrations/frequencies and music. This also made drastic changes in the water crystal's structure.

His conclusion was that different kinds of vibration have a certain effect on the molecular structure. You could say to yourself—well, it's only water. But remember, your body is about 60 percent or 90 percent water, depending on the study and the source of your information. The fact is still the same. Certain vibrations have a physical effect on matter, and your thoughts send out those vibrations. So, when you are thinking negative thoughts, it not only affects your own well-being, but will even affect your environment, your reality. We will look closer into this later.

While we are on the subject of the power of vibrations, I would like to bring to your attention to the forgotten genius—Royal Raymond Rife (May 16, 1888–August 5, 1971).

In the 1920s, Royal Raymond Rife had possibly made one of the most important medical discoveries in our known history. However, Rife's discoveries seem to be all forgotten. It's like the information was lost in time. It is also said that the American Medical Association destroyed and suppressed his technology. I don't want to go into conspiracy theories. However, do some research—you will be intrigued and you can make your own judgment.

Royal Raymond Rife invented the Rife machine. It was a way to selectively kill viruses and bacteria in a human body. He discovered that every virus and bacteria have its own life frequency or vibration. After mapping out these frequencies, Rife built a machine that projects energy (frequencies) into the body. As a result, the bacteria or virus in question started resonating and even exploded at the right frequency, just like glass does if you play a high enough frequency. Rife successfully treated viruses and bacteria with this machine, and Resonance Therapy was born. He also went on to test the machine with cancer patients. In one of his studies, he took 16 fatal cancer patients and treated them with the Rife machine on a cancer frequency. The cancer was simply destroyed and no trace was left. According to Rife, the success rate was 100 percent. It brings me back to this, and I hope you are starting to understand that everything is energy, and this energy has its own vibrational frequency.

If we tune into the right frequency, anything is possible. The vibrations we are transmitting create the reality we live in by actually affecting the atoms around us, depending on the frequency we are sending out.

Amazing, right? Energy can influence all other energy. You can influence the world around you. You need to look and understand this new way of viewing your reality. It opens our eyes to what our thoughts are really capable of, and how much power they have. When we take control of our thoughts, we can use them to attract the life we want.

Small shifts in your thinking and small changes in your energy can lead to massive alterations of your end result.—Kevin Michel.

The atoms or elementary particles themselves are not real; they form a world of potentialities or possibilities rather than one of things or facts.—Werner Heisenberg.

If I have got your attention, turn to chapter two, because the only person that can change your life is you.

CHAPTER 2

THE LAW OF VIBRATION

THE LAW OF VIBRATION HAS helped me shed some light on understanding how our reality is created and how our universe works.

Once we understand how everything, and I mean everything, is connected, only then can we move forward.

I believe this is the second stage of understanding of what we are and what our real potential is.

When we understand these principles, we set in motion a new belief system and a higher level of self-awareness. When our self-awareness rises, we start to take control of our lives. Remember, the stronger our foundation, the higher we can go.

We, as free-thinking human beings, have the ability and the power to change our lives. We can make our desires manifest into the material world! Sounds crazy, I know, but trust me, anybody who got anywhere in life, either consciously or unconsciously used this principle. Just like all of the laws of the universe, it is always present.

An example of this is, we don't see gravity but we know it is there, and we understand why it is there. My hope is, soon you will understand the law of vibration in the same way. Like everything we do in life, we must start at the bottom and work our way up. We first learn to walk before we learn to run. Every aspect of learning is done progressively.

All the information in this book connects the new scientific findings with ancient and spiritual beliefs. As the scientific minds grow more knowledgeable, we start to connect the dots and the missing links. What we see is that ancient civilizations and their belief systems, some going back over 9,000 years ago, are now only just being proven by the scientific community. Advancements in technology show us that the ancients understood the workings of the universe, and some of the teachings we follow today have been greatly derived from what they were talking about thousands of years ago.

It amazes me that this knowledge seems to have gone pretty unheard of, and we sure as hell don't see it in the mainstream media or schools. If you want to know about this research and information, you have to go looking for it.

There are many enlightened people and some great scientific minds trying to bring this information into the mainstream. However, unfortunately I, like most people didn't pay attention before. Life simply keeps us busy, and rarely do we question what we are taught. With the words "Seek and you shall find" echoing in my head, I did just that.

For everyone who asks receives; he who seeks finds; and to him who knocks, the door will be opened—Matthew 7:8.

In modern times, the Law of Vibration might not be as well-known as the Law of Attraction. However, the Law of Vibration serves as the foundation for the Law of Attraction. There are references throughout history about it, some in many ancient writings on wisdom, even though referred to as knowledge from the gods; you can find it in all modern-day religions and philosophies.

My understanding is that no matter how far you look back, you will find the same teachings and patterns. I decided to take a research journey to understand this knowledge, a journey I happily took because it has been life-changing in so many ways.

The Law of Attraction was popularized by Rhonda Byrne with the movie and book *The Secret* back in 2006. I remember watching the movie, and straight after that I purchased the book. However, for those who haven't read it or seen the movie, it basically teaches us that anything you think and feel unconsciously or consciously over time will manifest into your reality. I personally believe that *The Secret* is only a good introduction to a part of the subject. I have found later on that much information was missing; the book seems to only scratch the surface. But the principles and concepts are there.

I would recommend that you watch it or read it. I'm sure it will help you on your way. It's a good introduction to positive thinking and, as you will learn later, this is a very important key factor when we want to change our lives.

The Law of Attraction, which uses the power of the mind, states that what we think about our dominant thoughts when focused and backed by our own belief will translate and materialize into our reality. A basic explanation is, all thoughts turn into things eventually. Or, what we focus on consciously or unconsciously, we will create in our lives. If you focus on negative things, you will remain in a negative state of mind, thereby attracting more negative outcomes in your life.

But if you focus on positive thoughts and have a major goal or a burning desire that you are 100 percent focused on achieving, the universe will find a way for you to achieve it.

So now you must be wondering, how is all this possible?

You will soon come to understand, it is not how things will happen but the power and frequency of the vibration you are sending out. This is the way the universe works. I have read and researched just about everything I can get my hands on regarding the subject and I am constantly learning more, but to truly understand it we must trace back the information and teachings as far as we can go.

What you will find is that before the law of attraction it was the teachings of the law of vibration, and these teachings have been around even before the religions we worship and believe in today.

Soon you will understand how it is all connected. It is just a matter of perspective. In short, it will show you that we all have the unique power to create positive change in our reality. This power is nothing new. It has always been there, and those who understand it, use it. All Power Comes from Within.

PART 1: WHAT IS THE LAW OF VIBRATION?

First, let us look at the definition of the word Vibration concerning this context.

Vi·bra·tion: A person's emotional state, the atmosphere of a place, or the associations of an object, as communicated to and felt by others. Source: *The Encyclopedia and Oxford Dictionary*. Meaning we are sending and receiving vibrations all the time. The attraction is a law but this is only the secondary law; the primary and first law is the law of vibration. It is said that the law of vibration is one of the basic laws of the universe. It shows us that everything moves, nothing rests, our reality is an ocean of motion. A good example is that everything is simply an expression of the same thing—the leaves, the trees, the buildings, the human body, and even the clothes you wear—are all made of the same stuff. ENERGY

When we look at it on a subatomic level, it's all just a field or wave of energy and the only difference between them is the rate of vibration and frequency.

As I explained in chapter one, science has shown us through Quantum Physics that everything in our universe is energy and our thoughts and feelings have their own unique vibrational frequency. The actions we choose, the way we feel, all have their particular rates of vibration. Meaning your thoughts are inseparably connected to the rest of the universe and, as commonly said, "Like attracts like." Positive energies attract positive energies and negative energies attract negative energies. Have you ever noticed that people who are depressed keep being depressed and, on the other hand, happy people keep being happy? Have you ever wondered why some people are successful while others fail? We have the belief that some people are simply born lucky while others are not.

There is that old saying we use when referring to somebody that everything he touches turns to gold.

You will soon learn that it has nothing to do with luck, it is simply a state of mind. What vibrations we send out is what we get back. Like attracts like. There are always opposites. Happy/sad, successful/unsuccessful just like light and dark, positive and negative, hot and cold. It's always present; the only difference between everything is the frequency of vibration.

For example, the visible light frequency is from about 380 to 750 terahertz. The colors we see all have their own frequency. Just like heat, cold has its own frequency. Everything is simply a vibration of frequency—that means you, too!! Especially your emotions. This is easier to understand if you consider that when we go down on a subatomic level, we don't find matter, but pure energy. Some call this the Unified Field of the universe, meaning that anything that exists in or out of our universe, whether we can see it or not, if we break it down to the subatomic level and analyze it in its most basic form, it consists only of pure energy and that pure energy is vibrations. Nothing is solid, it is a vibratory frequency and everything is connected.

Now let me put a picture in your mind. If you throw a stone into the water, when the stone hits the water you would see perfectly formed ripples that will all move outward in the water. These are simply vibrations. Now let's think about you and your thoughts. When you think a thought, you are sending out a vibration just as the stone did in the water, they traveled outward into the universe field, and it is important for you to understand that you attract back to your vibrations similar to those you are sending out. That, in turn, will manifest as your circumstances in your life. We will look at this later, but right now just realize that everything is vibration, and everything is connected.

If you want to find the secrets of the universe, think in terms of energy, frequency, and vibration. — Nikola Tesla.

PART 2: THE HISTORY OF THE LAW OF VIBRATION

Back in 391 BC, the famous Greek philosopher Plato noted in his works that "likes tend towards likes." As you can see, I hope, by now, this is extremely close to the slogan "like attracts like."

Some of the early teachings on the subject have been put together and can be found in *The Kybalion: Hermetic Philosophy*, published back in 1908 by persons under the pseudonym of "the Three Initiates." They say that this book is the essence of the teachings of Hermes Trismegistus.

Now Hermeticism is a tradition that dates back as far as the first and second centuries AD. It is thought to be one of the oldest non-Christian belief systems. It is also said that these teachings have inspired and influenced many philosophers and artists of many generations. The same teachings can be traced back over 7,000 years to the ancient Egyptian, Grecians, and also the Vedic traditions of India.

On my journey, I have also found documents stating that there are great organizations of power out there, like the Freemasons and "the Order of the Skull and Bones," which discovered these teachings, and the information is only available to a select few or degree of membership in these organizations. It can also be found that great world leaders, royal families, and men in power have also accessed this information like it is a big secret. However, that could all be some kind of conspiracy theory. I have not found any reliable evidence on that, so we will stick to what is available.

As above, so below, as within, so without, as the universe, so the soul . . . .—Hermes Trismegistus.

So, 7,000 years ago the ancients used 7 universe laws.

What were these teachings based on?

In the *Kybalion*, each chapter is focused on its seven principles that are also considered as the universal laws from ancient times.

The 7 laws are as follows:

The Principle of Mentalism

The Principle of Correspondence

The Principle of Vibration

The Principle of Polarity

The Principle of Rhythm

The Principle of Causality

The Principle of Gender

But for this book and chapter, let's focus on law number three— THE PRINCIPLE OF VIBRATION.

This principle teaches us that "everything is in motion"; "everything vibrates"; "nothing is at rest"—facts that only now modern science is starting to prove to be correct. And yet this Hermetic

Principle was introduced thousands of years ago in ancient Egypt and Greece. The principle teaches us that the different manifestations of matter, energy, and mind result greatly from different rates of vibration. Look at it this way—if you change your mental state, you change your vibration. By changing your own vibration, you will change and shape your reality.

Nothing rests; everything moves; everything vibrates.

Throughout religious teachings, we can see a common golden thread that connects to everything you have read so far. I do not believe for one second that it is a coincidence that this information has been in front of us all the time. It's just a matter of perspective.

However, the ancients knew things that science today is proving to be possible; pretty amazing if you ask me.

Let us look at it on the timeline scale. Most religions date back around 2,500 years ago, give or take, whereas human civilization goes back about 300,000 years depending on your source of information.

My point is that many belief systems and religions have come and gone over 300,000 years but if we dig a little and research all sources of information, we can find a lot of similarities in their teachings. I also believe that many writings can be misinterpreted and lost over time. Whatever we believe to be true at the core, the most important thing is that if we are positive thinking beings, positive vibrations are sent outward, in turn, into the universe.

So, let's look at the similarities, let's look at the principle of "what we think we become" and "our thoughts create our reality."

The Hindu concept of Karma states that "Whatever you say or do, good or bad, will eventually return to you."

Also, the Bible (Galatians 5:6) says, "Whatsoever a man soweth, that shall he also reap."

In the writings about Jesus, it also spoke of the power we have to create when we employ the law. "Therefore, I say unto you, what things whatsoever ye desire, when ye pray, believe that ye receive them, and ye shall have them."—Mark 11:24

And again in the book of Matthew, "Ask, and it shall be given you; seek, and ye shall find; knock, and it shall be opened unto you." And, "And all things, whatsoever ye shall ask in prayer, believing, ye shall receive."

In Buddhism, we will find the words of Buddha. "All that we are is the result of what we have thought. The mind is everything. What we think we become." Here is another interesting fact—in the fourth century, the early Roman church removed a lot of the writings and scriptures from what we call the Bible today. It is said that the original teachings were more than 79 books. But biblical history is so argued over and so complicated that it is near impossible to say what the original Bible was or what it actually said.

But as my research on the subject has shown, a great amount of the writings has been removed. They even tried to destroy these teachings. However, some of them survived when they were discovered in Egypt back in 1945, also known as the Nag Hammadi library dating back to the 300 BC. It is a collection of thirteen ancient books (called "codices") in which the lost Gospel of

Thomas can be found. I think the passages in the scriptures are of great meaning in context with this book.

The Kingdom is inside of you and it is outside of you.—Gospel of Thomas

Recognize what is in your sight, and that which is hidden from you will become plain to you. For there is nothing hidden that will not become manifest.—Gospel of Thomas

What you seek after (is) within you.—The Dialogue of the Savior

That which you have will save you if you bring it forth from yourselves.—Gospel of Thomas

Now if we read these passages over and over again, we can start to see how it all connects.

It states EXACTLY what the law of vibration was trying to teach us, that you are the one with the power, you and only you control the outcome all the power is inside of you—thoughts + emotions = manifestation. When your thoughts and emotions combine, you get feelings. It is those feelings that send out the vibration to the universe. Then we are simply back to the meaning of we attract what we feel, our dominant thoughts.

MOVING FORWARD

As we move forward in time, we can find some great authors who have studied the subject and used the teachings in their self-development books.

They have used their own understanding of this ancient knowledge to enrich people's lives, teaching us the difference between happiness and sadness, success and failure, and how to improve our everyday lives. The following are some interesting insights into the books that have helped and guided me on my way. There are some amazing books out there that I would like to highlight.

They are what I would call important reads. Many authors wrote their books on similar kinds of principals. They had an understanding of the power of the human mind. I would highly recommend you find the time to read these books as well. At the end of this book, I will leave some recommendations for you. There is some amazing information stored in their pages.

I don't want you to think I am just doing a book review, but you will see why I wish to mention them to you. The connection of information can be found everywhere. My main point is, it all goes back to the law of vibration, and its teachings and principles can be found everywhere. The problem is when never realize until we start to understand the code of information.

Early in the 1900s, Wallace D. Wattles wrote one of the greatest books of his time, *The Science of Getting Rich*. Wattles practiced and believed in something he called creative visualization, which is still used today. We will look deeper into this method later on because it is an astonishing practice.

There are some very good success stories, my own included, which have used his very powerful technique and it is also used in most law of attraction teachings.

For those who are not familiar with his work, in a nutshell, he said that he formed a visual image or a mental picture in his mind of the thing or circumstances he wanted to manifest into his reality. He felt the feeling of gratitude as if it was already achieved. He would simply work toward his mental picture by taking positive action.

The following statement is from the *Science of Getting Rich* network:

"His daughter Florence once said, 'He wrote almost constantly. It was then that he formed his mental picture. He saw himself as a successful writer, a personality of power, an advancing man, and he began to work toward the realization of this vision.'"

The very best thing you can do for the whole world is to make the most of yourself.—Wallace D. Wattles.

A thought is a substance, producing the thing that is imagined by the thought.—Wallace D. Wattles.

James Allan: Back in 1903, James Allan wrote a book called *As a Man Thinketh*. James Allan was an Englishman who had the strong belief that both the conscious mind and subconscious mind have the power to create the reality around us, I also thought the title of this little 22-page book was interesting due to the fact that it was influenced by a verse in the Bible, "As a man thinketh in his heart, so is he." The conclusion that Allen gets to in this book is that "We do not attract what we want, but what we are."

Self-control is a strength. Right thought is mastery. Calmness is power.—James Allen.

The outer conditions of a person's life will always be found to be harmoniously related to his inner state...Men do not attract that which they want, but that which they are.—James Allen.

Charles F. Haanel, also known as the "Father of Personal Development," was the author of the book *The Master Key System*, which was published back in 1912. When I read *The Master Key System*, it was like going back to school. The book is laid out in 24 parts, starting at the basic parts of his philosophy and teachings, and advancing as you read, going into great detail. I guess that is where I got my ideas from for formulating this book for you.

The book is presented in a way that it teaches us about life and success while giving us the tools to use our powers in positive thinking. It shows us that we can control our circumstances and we can make our desires and dreams come true. By all means it is not an easy read, but when you get the grasp of it and the way it is written, it's mind-blowing. It is one of the most influential books I have read.

All thought is a form of energy, a rate of vibration, but a thought of the Truth is the highest rate of vibration known and consequently destroys every form of error in the same way that light destroys darkness; no form of error can exist when the "Truth" appears, so that your entire mental work consists in coming into an understanding of the Truth. This will enable you to overcome every form of lack, limitation or disease of any kind.—Charles F. Haanel

Before we move on, there are a lot of amazing authors out there I could mention. However, one has always stood out more than the rest for me and his books and teachings have shaped the lives of millions; even to this day, almost 100 years later, people still study his writings, with amazing results. This man brings a whole new meaning to the word Dedication.

That is Napoleon Hill, the author who wrote the first million-copy bestseller book on the subject of the law of attraction, *Think and Grow Rich*, in 1937. Hill dedicated more than 20 years of his life to study the world's richest and successful minds. He researched and interviewed more than 500 of the most successful people of his time, some of them we still recognize today, like Thomas Edison, Henry Ford, Charles M. Schwab, Alexander Graham Bell, President Theodore Roosevelt, and Andrew Carnegie. Hill also stated that the idea for the book *Think and Grow Rich* came from his interview with the world's richest man at the time—Andrew Carnegie. Hill believed that his knowledge was sacred, and that Andrew Carnegie wanted Hill to share this knowledge and understanding with the world.

Napoleon Hill also published a book called *How to Raise Your Own Salary*. It is said that the book is based on the interview dialog between Napoleon Hill and Andrew Carnegie from their meetings in 1908. There's also the story that Carnegie challenged Hill and said, if you dedicate your time I will introduce you to the greatest minds of our time, and you will learn the secrets to success that only a few men know. Hill later stated he also found the golden thread, the common factor that makes a man a success or a failure.

Andrew Carnegie (1835–1919)

For those of you who do not know who Andrew Carnegie was, he was one of the wealthiest businessmen of his time. He was a self-made steel tycoon and the founder of the Carnegie Steel Company. His company, by 1889, was recognized as the largest of its kind in the world. His background story, to cut it short, was that he had nothing when he started, he worked his way up through the world, and he had a great philosophy of life. He believed all men are self-made by the power of their minds and their habits. Here are some quotes from *How to Raise Your Own Salary*:

From what you say about habits, I have reached the conclusion that success is a habit.—Napoleon Hill

Now you are getting the idea! Of course, success is a habit.—Andrew Carnegie

Every man is where he is and what he is because of his own mental attitude as it is expressed through his personality.—Andrew Carnegie

What Hill discovered was that we can control our minds. We have the power to choose and control our thoughts—we can choose to use our thoughts constructively or negatively. By controlling our thoughts, we have the power to influence the world around us. You are your own master when you have a positive state of mind and definiteness of purpose or a major goal, and when we believe in ourselves and see our goal reached through the force of habit thinking, everything is possible.

Success comes to those who become success conscious. Failure comes to those who indifferently allow themselves to become failure conscious.—Napoleon Hill That before we can accumulate riches in great abundance, we must magnetize our minds with an intense desire for riches that we must become "money conscious" until the desire for money drives us to create definite plans for acquiring it.—Napoleon Hill, *Think and Grow Rich*

PART 3: WHAT DOES THE LAW MEAN FOR YOU?

As I come to wrap up this chapter, I will try to explain to you as I have come to see it. Once we come to understand that we are all vibrations of frequency, and our thoughts and emotions amplify those vibrations, we can then start to see a small part of how the universe works. We start to realize that this information is nothing new—it has always been there since the dawn of time.

We know that science can also document the effects our minds have on the world around us. Our thoughts are actual things. We are what we feel we are, from the way we walk and talk to the way we treat others, all this has effects on our personal reality. We start to see the possibilities that life can offer us as long as we are in the right frame of mind and understanding. We can control what we think and feel. The point is we need to become aware of it, and through habit and understanding we have the power to do just that. If you think and feel positive, your vibration will change. This will place before you opportunities and people that will enable you to achieve your goals and desires.

As simple as this—you are the painter of your own life what you paint on the canvas is your choice.

The Law of Vibration or the Law of attraction is really simple, just like all laws of nature. They are completely perfect. You must learn to hold onto the desired idea or situation you want in life, and if you can hold it there in the mind's eye and believe it has already been achieved, backed by faith, things in your life will start to change.

But it's not that easy, is it? I know that feelings of hopelessness and fear can quickly take control, and we need to understand why this brings me to the next stage of building your foundations stronger conscious vs the subconscious.

Get ready. It will be a bumpy ride.

CHAPTER 3

CONSCIOUS VS SUBCONSCIOUS

SO FAR, WE HAVE LOOKED at life on the quantum level, and I hope by now you have started to get a new understanding of how everything in the universe is connected.

When looking at some of the oldest belief systems and religions, we can start to see there is a connection between what they taught and what the latest scientific research is showing us. Their findings are the same as what the ancients said—everything is energy and everything vibrates at its own frequency.

Everything you are, down to the smallest particle, is simply energy.

Each thought we have has its own vibration and it has become clear in modern-day psychology that our thoughts and feelings are what controls us and actions in our daily lives. That being said, it is only logical that if we want great change in our lives, we must learn and understand how to control these thoughts and emotions. When we can do this, then our potential for greater quality of life can be achieved. But we are crazy and complicated thinking beings, and we now know that we are all made of the same stuff but unfortunately our results in life can be drastically different.

So why is it then that some people are happy while others are depressed? Why do some people believe in one thing and others completely deny it?

Why is it that people get stuck in the same old routines and habits and never really seem to get anywhere in life?

Why do some people succeed and some fail? Why is it that some people think positive and others think negative?

There seems to be an understandable science behind all these whys. Have you ever noticed that some of us have this reach-for-the-stars kind of attitude and believe anything is possible while others simply accept life's circumstances? They just seem to give up or believe there's no point to even try anymore.

They become locked in this negative way of thinking, and the real problem is that they probably don't even realize they're doing this to themselves. If you believe, for example, that you can't do something or it's not possible, then you will not be able to do it even though that is completely not true. It's your own belief that holds you back.

WHY? Because without the right mind-set and beliefs, you will not get anywhere in life. Everything will simply stay the same. If you keep thinking what you have always been thinking, you will keep getting the same results.

Instead of moving forward in life, you will stay in the same status you are now, so yesterday will be the same as tomorrow. Your beliefs and thoughts are what drive you or hold you back. Without the right understanding and motivation, you're just stuck in the moment with no final destination in sight.

It's just like a car without the engine or the plane without the pilot. They will simply stand still; nothing will change until you change yourself from within.

You need to put the engine in the car—the driving mechanism, the belief.

You need to put the pilot in the plane. Take control of your mind and know where you want to go. One thing I have observed, and I'm sure you have too, is that people who are unhappy with their life or circumstances in their life could give you a thousand or even a million reasons why they're not where they want to be in life. Most people will have some kind of excuse or belief that someone or some experience made it impossible for them to succeed. People can always find something to blame for their misfortunes or chances lost in life. Unfortunately, it becomes like a story they tell themselves and others, and that story repeats itself daily. That's why nothing changes in their lives—they are living in the same story over and over.

It's a hard truth to understand. Of course, there are experiences that could have been out of their control. But we all have the ability to think and understand how we can learn to deal with these thoughts and emotions afterward. First, we need to understand how the mind works. It is also important to know that those emotions are the vibrations we are sending out to the world. Like attracts like or negative attracts negative. Sorry I keep repeating myself, but soon you will understand why! Hey, at the end of this chapter remember this quote—It's not my fault but my responsibility.

The common truth is, no matter how we look at the human mind, we should understand it is the creator of our reality. I know this is hard to grasp right now, but stay with me, when I personally came to understand this great principle and started to believe in my own power of thought, my life's circumstances started to change. I became aware of my emotional status, and how my negative thoughts crept in, and how these thoughts affected my views on life and the world around me. But over time, with a positive habit of thinking and greater awareness of how my own mind works, my results in life started to change. The simple information in this chapter will give you more control and understanding of what you need to do to change your life for the better, starting from within.

Ninety-nine percent of the failures come from people who have the habit of making excuses.—George Washington Carver

The human mind is the creator of both positive and negative, and the words positive and negative can be used in so many contrasts, for example, success or failure, motivated or inactive, ambitious or ambitionless.

Your mind is a powerful piece of biological equipment. It is capable of so much. The human mind is the great designer of both creation and destruction.

Think about this for a moment. Everything you take for granted, from the car you drive, the house you live in, to the great skyscrapers, and other great achievements of structural ingenuity; every piece of technology you use—computers, smartphones, even the electricity that lights our cities, the medical equipment that saves lives every day; the literature you read and learn from—everything originally came from someone's mind. Their mind has been responsible for many positive inventions, from the light bulb, the telephone, to the airplane—and there are a billion more—which have bettered the lives of humankind. But on the other side of the scale, we can see the negative results of the mind—the weapons of war, the guns, atomic bombs, nuclear missiles, chemical warfare, all man-made devices—it all came from somebody's thoughts. Whether it's positive or negative, when the idea is born in the mind, sooner or later the mind finds a way to make it become a material thing, so it's true if we say "From the mind into reality."

Everything we know comes from a lot of human minds developing their own ideas and visions. I now see it like this—we are all creative beings with endless potential both for good and for evil, positive or negative, whatever you would like to call it. The end result is the same—that our thoughts create our reality, whether we are aware of it or not. The only difference is the way the human mind is used. For generations, man has tried to define what the mind is and how it really works. There is growing evidence that connects to the ancient beliefs that the mind goes beyond the physical structure of the brain and body, and that everything in the universe is connected. So, it's important for us to understand

and get our thinking under control. Your thoughts and feelings and your beliefs all cause you to behave and act the way you do.

An interesting finding is that scientists and psychologists have stated that 95 percent of our thoughts are the same ones we had yesterday. We get stuck in a kind of thought loop without ever being aware of it.

So, it all comes down to this—if you want to change your life, you need to understand your thoughts and beliefs. Many great minds have stated along these terms—all great achievement starts within, or the secret to life is truly to know oneself and one's own power.

So, let's get down to business! Let's look at how it all comes together. Let's understand why we think and feel the way we do. Once we have this understanding, our foundations get stronger!

He who knows others is wise; he who knows himself is enlightened.—Lao Tzu.

Your own Self-Realization is the greatest service you can render the world.—Ramana Maharshi.

No one is free who has not obtained the empire of himself. No man is free who cannot command himself.—Pythagoras.

PART 1: CONSCIOUS VS SUBCONSCIOUS

There are two basic areas of the human mind—the conscious and the subconscious. The subconscious can process 40 million bits of data from the world around you every second. While the front part of your brain, called consciousness, can process only 50 bits of data per second. This will show you that the subconscious mind is 1 million times more powerful than the conscious mind.

The famous Sigmund Freud (1856–1939), the Austrian Psychoanalyst, came up with a great way to visualize the human mind. He said if we think of an iceberg to describe the two parts of the human mind, the tip of the iceberg that is above the water represents your conscious mind, while the larger part of the iceberg that is under the water represents your subconscious mind.

This explanation shows that the conscious mind is only the tip of the iceberg.

Consciousness?

For generations, the world's most intelligent minds have tried to explain what consciousness really is. There have been many theories on the subject, but one fact remains—the human mind is always developing. We have gone from early caveman to what we call modern man today. The mind has developed in an evolution kind of sense. We have learned and expanded our knowledge and awareness over thousands of years. Consciousness simply means that we are aware, that we are alive, and we are aware of the environment around us. Consciousness is your individual awareness of everything you have experienced and your present moment, the here and now. Without consciousness we would not exist, because if we did exist, we would not know it. Consciousness reminds you that you exist.

The conscious mind is associated with who and what you are. It is the conscious mind that communicates with the world around you.

It is the source of thought. It uses all your senses and makes all the daily decisions. It is your real-time awareness. It is the part of the mind that is responsible for your creativity and your command to speak and move. It basically controls all the actions that you do intentionally. Your conscious mind is like the general of an army giving orders and commands to your body to get things done or expressed in some way.

It is also like the keeper at the gate, because your conscious mind also acts like a filter, stopping information before it reaches the subconscious mind. For example, if you are presented with new information that does not match your beliefs, the conscious mind will simply filter it out or discard it before it can reach your subconscious mind.

This brings me to the most important part of the mind . . . the part of the mind we need to focus on understanding the most— the subconscious mind.

True philosophy must start from the most immediate and comprehensive fact of consciousness: I am life that wants to live, in the midst of life that wants to live.—Albert Schweitzer.

Subconscious?

You would like to think that you are in complete control of your thoughts and life. However, most of what we do act and feel is due to years of programming in the subconscious mind.

It is very important you understand this. Your beliefs create your thoughts, your thoughts control your emotions, and your emotions have an effect on how you present yourself to the world around you. The beliefs you have and the interpretations you have, including the way you view yourself and your opinions on life are all due to the hardwired subconscious.

Yes, I said the words programming and hardwired for a reason, because I can't find a more realistic meaning. The subconscious is just like a computer. It starts getting programmed from the day you are born, and the programming stays there, hardwired, unless you develop the skills to reprogram your subconscious.

Let me explain.

From day one of your life, the subconscious has been busy recording information—some of this through experiences and some of it from what has been given to you in the form of information—and your subconscious never sleeps; it's always at work. When you were young your subconscious was like a sponge, absorbing everything—because you had no existing beliefs to contradict what you were learning, everything must be true. That's why a child's mind is so full of fantasy and so easily programmed. When you have reached the age of seven or eight, you already have your core beliefs set in stone; all this is due to the programming from mum and dad, or people in your life—what they say and do, you observe, and this becomes a part of your belief system.

Since day one you have been told what to eat, what to wear, what was right, and what was wrong. Everything around had some kind of effect on you—from the environment you grow up in, even the television shows you watched, all had an effect on your subconscious mind. Now the subconscious doesn't know what's right or wrong, fantasy or real. It simply accepts the beliefs until challenged.

Everything you are is because of the subconscious mind.

Think about the religious man or woman. They believe that their religion is the right one and all others must be false, for the simple fact that that is how they were programmed earlier on in life. In the history books, we see entire civilizations going to war over their beliefs, and it takes generations to reprogram these old beliefs.

I need one of those baby monitors from my subconscious to my consciousness so I can know what the hell I'm really thinking about.—Steven Wright

The subconscious mind's main job is to store and retrieve data when needed. You respond in situations exactly to your default program. Everything you say and do is because of your programming. Your subconscious mind has been programmed by habit. Everything you have done over and over again eventually becomes the program. Remember how you learned how to ride a bike? You never forgot that, did you?

Every day you tie your shoes. You never forgot how to, did you?

Your sense of danger, whether it is water, fire, great heights, etc., they have always been present.

You now have a sense of danger. This was taught to you at a very early age, whereas a small child's mind has no sense of danger until told through habit. Simply because the subconscious remembers everything that has been experienced and said to you through habit and repetition, it stores the information that it thinks is important for future use. Whatever you do over and over again, or whatever you have been told over and over, the subconscious mind will accept the information as true whether it is or not. The subconscious mind is always present, and it is your autopilot, both in your thoughts and actions, that is steering the ship the only way it knows.

I'm sure you can find many examples in your own life where the subconscious simply takes over. For example:

Have you ever been having a conversation while driving your car? Your conscious mind is focusing on the conversation and your subconscious mind takes care of the driving without you even realizing. Your subconscious mind is your protector. It will always step in at great times of danger and it puts your body into survival mode. It will do whatever it can to keep you alive.

There is a lot of evidence out there regarding the power of the subconscious mind. Stories of people lifting great heavy objects to save their children without even realizing it, like they had some kind of superhuman strength. The subconscious mind simply took over, to do what was needed to be done. Your mind is a powerful thing.

Another great example of this is, right now you are using your conscious mind to read this book. However, behind the scenes your subconscious mind is busy at work sorting out this information. Accepting it or rejecting it is all based on your existing perception on what is right or wrong. You see it's always there, it's always present, and without it we would be dead already. It keeps your body in constant check, it keeps your body at just the right temperature—98.6 degrees—it keeps your heart pumping, it keeps you breathing, and sends a million other messages to the body. Everything you need to do in order to stay alive, the subconscious has control.

It is important from here on that you understand this—your subconscious mind is responsible for 95 percent to 99 percent of what you do and what you believe, and feel it all comes from your default program. It is a warehouse of information and it uses your memories, both positive and negative, to guide you on through life. This is where all your habits and beliefs come from.

I'll say it one more time just in case you missed it! The subconscious mind is the autopilot of your mind.

Man moves in a world that is nothing more or less than his consciousness objectified.—Neville Goddard

PART 2: THE POWER OF AUTO-SUGGESTION

Now, remember your subconscious is always recording, so the following information is a key factor if we are going to understand how it all works.

SUGGESTION—

A suggestion is the most powerful thing, I have discovered, when it comes to our subconscious mind. The reason I say this is that all your mental limitations in life are due to suggestions and your own personal beliefs. Your views on money and wealth are due to suggestion. For example, if you were taught in your earlier years that money does not grow on trees and times are hard, or money is the root of all evil, you will go through life with this belief because of these suggestions. It's all about your mind-set.

Majority of children coming from successful families have an imprint of success from an early age, and strive to be like their family or the people that influenced them early on in life. Wherever you look, in all social groups, you will see the same kind of pattern or a very high percentage of people doing the same as those around them do. Like the old saying goes, the apple doesn't fall very from the tree. There is another old saying I have heard a lot throughout my life and that is that the rich get richer and the poor get poorer. This is no coincidence. I'm afraid it's all about mindset. If you were told by children in your school days that you were ugly, stupid, lazy, it's possible that later on in life you would develop low self-esteem or lack of motivation due to the suggestions of others. Your subconscious stored this information and generated your thoughts about yourself or limitations.

Your mind is working on your future based on a suggestion. The question is on whose suggestion it's working on: Yours or others?—Assegid Habtewold.

Think about your own limitations or beliefs. Right now, they all come from some experience or somebody telling you. Just like in the last chapter, everything has a cause and an effect, whether we are aware of it or not. Suggestion is everywhere—from the TV shows we watch to the advertisements you see; everything is based on suggestion. Suggestion is the great power behind everything we do and everything we want. Unfortunately, many of us have been so used to seeing or hearing the negative side of suggestion we actually attract more of the same without even knowing it. We become programmed to a certain extent to look for it.

Your mind is attracted to what it is used to—for example, if you walk past a newspaper stand and the headlines say doomsday is coming, it gets your attention but if the headlines say it's a beautiful world, you would probably walk straight past without giving it a second thought.

Wherever you look in history, you can see this power of suggestion being used. A great example of this was in a book I read, called *The Magic of Believing*, by Claude M. Bristol.

In the book *The Magic of Believing*, Claude said, in Germany, during the World War II, Hitler understood the power of suggestion—everywhere you looked in Germany, you could see Hitler's image and slogans—Ein Volk, Ein Reich, Ein Fuhrer, meaning One People, One Nation, One Leader. It was a little bit like mass hypnosis. Getting people to believe and follow through repetition. We see the same type of tactics in modern times—with the news and media we get only a limited perspective of the world's events, and the information we receive is what forms our views and opinions. We see this power of suggestion everywhere we go—the advertising boards and big TV screens, in streets and cities, there's no escape. Even your social media sites are full of advertising.

Buy this product, drink this drink—it's everywhere, and it's constant because the people selling their products know that the more you see it and hear it, the more you are likely to buy it. One of the biggest industries in the world is the pharmaceutical industry. There is always some new miracle pill on the market or a medicine that will solve all your problems or take your pain away. My point is, the power of suggestion is very real and it is everywhere. You may not be consciously aware of it, but you are being bombarded with suggestive information all the time. It is a great power to those who know how to use it, and sooner or later all these types of suggestions, through repetition, will be absorbed into the subconscious mind.

AUTO-SUGGESTION—

Now we get to the good stuff. This is a big part of the book's title—*What Happens Next Changes Everything.*

Your major beliefs, which influence your thoughts and personality, as you have just read, are all due to your childhood years of programming. As if that was not bad enough, on top of this, through the power of suggestion, we are constantly being told what to think. This just goes to show how little control we really have.

So, in order to rewrite this, we must constantly introduce new ideas and a new belief system, and the only way we can do this is through auto-suggestion.

Auto-suggestion is the way you can influence the good old subconscious mind. It basically means self-suggestion and, through repetition and habit, we can find a way into the subconscious. Your mind, yes yours, is just like your computer. It has been running on the default program. Your personality, your attitude, your current status in life, are all due to your default program. But what if we are not happy with this program? What if we realize we can be a better person and want a better life? In order for us to bring about change, we must use auto-suggestion.

If the power of suggestion wrote this program, it seems only natural that the power of suggestion can rewrite the program. This is where auto-suggestion comes in.

The power of thought, the idea, is incommensurable, is immeasurable. The world is dominated by thought.—Emile Coué

But first we need to understand the effects of auto-suggestion. All your life you have been using auto-suggestion, whether you realize it or not. Most of us do it unconsciously. It has always been present, especially in your attitude, and often this is what is stopping us from accomplishing the life we want. You can see it in your limitations, even in your health, the power of auto-suggestion is always present. Whatever you are constantly telling yourself will, of course, have an effect on who you are. We can all find excuses, or someone to blame, but that will not change the subconscious mind. You are only reinforcing your beliefs, your default program.

We can also say it's not my fault because of this and that. Whatever you think, it will only justify your status in life. It is simply your old beliefs repeating themselves. It is your subconscious mind out of control. As we said earlier, 95 percent of your thoughts are the same ones you had yesterday.

The subconscious mind cannot move outside its fixed pro-grams—it automatically reacts to situations with its previously stored behavior responses.—Bruce Lipton

Positive examples of auto-suggestion—I can ride that bike; I have done it before. I can do it, I will get that job, I always do. My body is always in perfect health, it's my genetics.

Negative examples of auto-suggestion—I can't do it. I will never have that house. I'm tired all the time, I'm stressed. If only I had that job. I'm sick all the time. My body is broken. People are talk-ing about me. Constantly complaining, blaming others—I'm sick and tired all the time, life's hard, I'm unlucky.

You are what you say you are. The problem is, we get stuck in this destructive routine of thinking, and the worst part about it is that over time it becomes a habit and then unconsciously we keep doing the same thing. It becomes the main program. Have you ever noticed how successful people keep being successful and people who are broke stay broke, and people who are con-stantly complaining about their health are constantly sick and seem to have constant health problems? Well, there is a reason for this, and by now you should be starting to understand why! Auto-suggestion. You are what you say you are. If you constantly see negative thoughts and put limitations on yourself, you are sending that message backed by your emotions to your subconscious. The subconscious mind does not know what is, true or false. It simply is.

Through the constant repetition of these emotions and thoughts, they will be stored away in that great warehouse of information—your subconscious—and, in turn, become your default program.

Marcus Aurelius, the great Roman Emperor, said: "A man's life is what his thoughts make of it."

AWARENESS OF SUGGESTION

The basic principle you need to know in order to use auto-suggestion to your benefit is that we must be aware of our own thoughts, and learning how to control them is the main essential. You need to stop yourself thinking negative. You need to tell yourself, through the habit of thinking, stop, I will only focus on the positive. Also, in life, in any given situation, there is a small amount of time when the emotion of the situation hits you. This small window of time is where your level of awareness of suggestion comes in. In chapter six, all this will become clear, so, for now, we will only touch on the subject of awareness.

When you become self-aware of the power of suggestion, you can start to control how you are going to express yourself in the outer world. For this, you must become a master of remembering that our attitude toward life is life's attitude toward us, try to only let words of positiveness come out. I remember the old saying that if you have nothing positive to say then don't say anything unless you can do it in a constructive way.

Don't talk about ill-health. We don't need sympathy. We need a positive mental attitude and a positive picture of ourselves.

Don't mention the lack of money, replace it with words like "I attract abundance," "Things are changing for the better." There is an old saying, fake it until you make it. And it could not be further from the truth just believe and feel it as was all ready here.

Most of your daily thinking is automatically negative. Worrying about money, worrying about this and that, etc.—when you put focus on these negative perceptions or emotions, you are simply sending out the vibrations on the negative frequency, and this will attract more of the same vibrations.

Remember you are the product of your thoughts and your environment. The subconscious is automatic, and once programmed you go into AUTOPILOT. If you want to really change this, you need to have new goals, new ways of thinking, new ways to control your emotions and your default reactions.

You need to become self-aware of all of the above. And most of all, you must believe that you can change. This is how to use the power of auto-suggestion to your advantage. Later on in this book, we put all this information together. Then you will have your own master plan and the tools you need to put everything into practice. However, right now we gotta keep working on those foundations.

If you want a change in your life you must believe it's possible, you must have faith in you, only you have control of the outcome.— Harley Hanson

You can't control what people say, but you can control your own thoughts. Let it go, give it no attention. Negative thinking only attracts more negative thinking. Remember that the next time somebody pisses you off.

Before we move to the next chapter, I would like to bring to your attention something I recommend you do before you read any further. It has to be one of the most amazing and influential recordings I have ever heard, and the man behind it is a true icon in the world of self-development.

So, let me tell you why . . .

I did not want to write too personally in this book but this situation is relevant to this chapter and I stumbled upon this recording back in 2008. I was going through a rough time in my life and my health was in very bad shape. I was fitted with a pacemaker to support my heart, at the same time I lost my job, and things were looking dull, you could say. But I have always been a strong-minded person and I know a solution would present itself and, in a strange way, it did. Not long after, I was up and on the go again. I was driving along in my car, playing some music from my phone on YouTube. As the song finished, it automatically went over to the next video. However, it was not a song, it was an old recording by Earl Nightingale called *The Strangest Secret*. I was just about to reach down to my phone to skip it over. However, something told me to wait. It was a weird experience, so I listened, and straight after it finished, I listened again. Something hit me. It got me thinking about my own life. It all made sense to me. In his words I found a new understanding, and I was intrigued. Thinking back, it was that unexpected recording that started me on my journey. It was like the first stepping stone. You could say it got my wheels in motion.

It has been a great influence on my life. It answered many of my questions regarding life, and gave me the motivation to learn more. To this day I still listen to it at least twice a week. It helps keep me focused. It is the best form of suggestion I have found. I don't want to write about it because I would not do it the justice it deserves.

So, take a break and go to YouTube and listen to *The Strangest Secret* by Earl Nightingale. I'm sure the information in that old recording will make sense to you as well.

Whatever we plant in our subconscious mind and nourish with repetition and emotion will one day become a reality.—Earl Nightingale

Your past does not define you; you are only a product of your past. Because your subconscious is hardwired, your default program is playing. Whatever you believe to be true is true, so remember, the past is not your fault but the future is your responsibility. To change, all you need to do is believe—which takes us to the next chapter.

CHAPTER 4

THE POWER OF BELIEF

BY NOW YOU SHOULD HAVE a better understanding of how your mind works, and how the subconscious mind impacts our daily lives. All your beliefs and automatic reactions and feelings come from your default program.

The conscious mind is responsible for thought and the actions you intend to do intentionally, whereas your subconscious mind is the source of all power. Your emotions and beliefs are all controlled by your subconscious mind.

You should also have a greater understanding of the power of suggestion and the meaning of auto-suggestion. Your default program is hardwired, and if you want to make a dramatic change in your life, you need to hack this program and create a new and better you. A positive program with no limitations.

Be a person who sets new goals and archives them with a positive mental attitude towards life. You and only you can change the process of negative thinking. You can lift yourself up to a higher level of consciousness by becoming aware of your thoughts and emotions. By doing this, you set in motion a way to change your default program.

Therefore, we must first understand how this is done, and then we must put it into practical use. Thoughts are nothing without action but, most importantly, you must believe in you.

To state it simply, Change Everything.

PART 1: BELIEVING IS POWER

Throughout our lives, we can see great evidence of how the power of belief works. We see it in all great human achievements and discoveries, we see it in the athlete, we can see it in the music industry, and it is always constant in the business world when related to success. Without belief, there is no achievement possible.

Belief is simply a frame of mind. It is the constant motivation to succeed. It is the ability of the mind not to accept failure and to push on, no matter the odds. It is what separates people of success or failure.

Beliefs can make a man great, and the same beliefs can destroy a man.

Beliefs can heal the body, and beliefs can also deteriorate the body.

Beliefs can hold you back, and beliefs can also push to great heights.

Whatever you believe to be true is true to you!

To believe in something, and not to live it, is dishonest.— Mahatma Gandhi.

The late Thomas Edison (1847–1931) well known as one of the world's greatest inventors, is a prime example of the power of belief. Edison now has over 1,000 patents, and is responsible for inventions like the typewriter, phonograph, and the motion picture camera. The most commonly known one is the light bulb. It is said that Edison failed in his experiments to invent the light bulb more than 10,000 times. However, through his constant **Persistence** and his own belief, the light bulb was created. He simply never gave up on his vision.

I have not failed. I've just found 10,000 ways that won't work.—Thomas A. Edison

Walt Disney—I'm pretty sure you have heard of him. Many of us grew up watching his cartoons on TV. Did you know that early on in life he was fired from his newspaper job? They said that he lacked imagination. He also went bankrupt several times. Guess what he had? A strong desire and he believed he could build something great.

Look where his belief got him.

Author J. K. Rowling was a struggling single mum living on welfare. She said, "In the beginning, I did not have much self-belief but I had this vision and that was one day I would become a great writer." She held onto that one belief and never gave up. Now she is the billionaire lady behind the successful Harry Potter empire.

Wherever we see someone's success, we see the same common factor—it does not matter where they come from, or their personal history. If they truly believe in themselves, anything is possible.

You can see it in every great athlete. They all have a common goal—to be the best they can be. They dedicate their time to improve their physical condition. They have the mind-set of reaching their goals, and those who don't, quit or get distracted before reaching it.

If my mind can conceive it if my heart can believe it—then I can achieve it.—Muhammad Ali

When a person has a strong faith, this faith is built upon a belief. The stronger their belief, the more dedication they show. In all faiths, we hear about miracles—people being cured of illnesses. People can go to these great congregations and be healed by faith healers. Science has shown us again and again that the actual healing had nothing to do with the healer, it was simply the person's faith and their own belief that it would work. Their bodies healed themselves through the power of belief.

In the province of the mind, what one believes to be true either is true or becomes true.—John Lilly

In the scientific world, there has been a great amount of study and research on what they call the placebo effect. The phenomenon occurs when someone is given a particular medication and told it is a cure for their health problems, even though the medication has no real substance—it is mostly just a sugar pill or something like that. However, the people taking this medication believe it is the cure for their illness.

The scientists have found the results to be outstanding! The patient is cured, their particular health problem has gone without any introduction of real medication. The findings simply tell us the role of the mind in health and well-being. There is great power in that and, by faith and belief, anything is possible.

People who are constantly worried about ill health usually find themselves with ill health problems. I don't think this is at all a coincidence. We go straight back to suggestion—whatever we put our focus on will be our outcome. Everywhere we look, there is talk about disease and scary new diseases. On TV, in newspapers—it's everywhere, and the truth is, if we think about it too much, we start to fear it. Which brings me to the conclusion that if the mind can heal the body through the power of belief, it only seems logical that the reverse is possible. It's just a matter of what we put our focus on.

The Power of Suggestion again!

There have been remarkable stories about cancer patients who were terminally ill but refused to accept their diagnoses. They told themselves they were cured, and believed 100 percent that they were going to live and everything was going to be ok. And the crazy thing is, the people in those documented cases were right—they healed themselves, with no explanation from their doctors regarding how this was even possible. Whatever the reasons are for these people to regain good health, I'm pretty sure the mind and their beliefs played a big part in their recovery.

Beliefs are everywhere, and beliefs are powerful things. In the old times, it was black magic and witch doctors, voodooism, and witches—wherever you look, you will find it is not the practice that has the power, it is the person's own belief that affects the outcome. Whatever you believe to be true long enough, eventually it will sink into your subconscious mind, creating a new thought process. That thought process then changes your vibration, and whatever your vibration is will show up in your experiences in the outer world.

I hope you are starting to see how this is all connected. Your beliefs drive your emotions, and the emotions control your actions and thoughts. It may be a lot to take in, but once you believe you have the power, and you find the motivation to change, change will follow.

PART 2: BELIEFS VS REALITY

Now you understand the power of your beliefs and how they can affect your mind and even your body. The beliefs you have—your core beliefs—all come from the subconscious mind. It is just as important to know that your subconscious mind does not know the difference between what is real and what is your imagination.

A good example of this can be found if we look at nightmares! When you're having a nightmare, a really bad one, your subconscious mind actually believes it's all real. All the physical symptoms are created—sweating, increased heart rate, body movements—it's not until you finally wake up that the conscious mind says, wait, wait, it is only a dream. Soon after, your body goes back into normal function. Another great example of this was in a scientific study to do with the power of the subconscious mind and the power of belief.

Richard Suinn, a sports psychologist, did experiments to try to show that the subconscious did not know what was real or unreal. In one experiment, he placed electrodes on the heads and bodies of elite skiers, and asked them to imagine certain ski courses and visualize they were doing them. What he found was that the brain sends electrical signals to the body that are comparable to what they would be if they were actually doing it. All this means that what we believe to be true is true. This is our individual reality.

The subconscious does not know what is real and what is imaginary.

Whatever you are thinking or telling yourself over and over again, whether it is true or not, will become your belief—the subconscious then believes it to be true. It will also work outside of your daily conscious awareness to prove your beliefs to be true. It believes this is what you want. Do you see the pattern now?

I hope it is all coming together for you. First, it was our programming that built up our beliefs. Then our beliefs dictated our results in life. When we look back on our own beliefs, they all come from the subconscious mind, and the subconscious does not know what is real. It does not know what is positive or negative. It acts on the belief alone.

It seems only logical that in order to change any negative belief, we must replace it with a positive one. We must truly believe in the thing we want to accomplish or the circumstances we want in our lives.

Life isn't about finding yourself. Life is about creating yourself.— George Bernard Shaw

But that's easier said than done, because our old routines of thinking and beliefs creep back in. Everyone, at some point in their lives, has set themselves a new goal or resolution. I'm sure you have been there. And you know what happens to that goal—nine out of ten times it simply fades away. That could take or a day or a few months, but usually we fall back into the same old routines. Like they say, old habits die hard. If we are not constantly giving awareness to our new beliefs and pushing them forward with motivation without any distractions, we will fall straight back into our old ways pretty fast.

Why? Because we lack imagination; we lack the vision of ourselves achieving the desired goal; we need to see ourselves at the finish line, and believe we can do it. Your own personal reality is yours to create. If you don't like your reality, then you must understand that you have the power to change it. The power is your power of belief—the more you believe anything is possible, the more things you can change. Belief is one of the keys to change everything.

It all comes down to this when you believe, and you imagine you can create. This brings us to the next chapter of Imagination. But before we move on, I have added the story of Thomas Edison, which demonstrates the power of belief. I think this is a prime example of belief.

One day Thomas Edison came home and gave a paper to his mother. He told her, "My teacher gave this paper to me and told me to only give it to my mother." His mother's eyes were tearful as she read the letter out loud to her child: Your son is a genius. This school is too small for him and doesn't have enough good teachers for training him. Please teach him yourself. Many years later, after Edison's mother died and he was now one of the greatest inventors of the century, one day he was looking through the old family things. Suddenly he saw a folded piece of paper in the corner of a drawer in a desk. He took it out and opened it up. On the paper was written: Your son is addled [mentally ill]. We won't let him come to school anymore.

Edison cried for hours, and then he wrote in his diary: "Thomas Alva Edison was an addled child that, by a hero mother, became the genius of the century."

CHAPTER 5

IMAGINATION

IMAGINATION—THE FACULTY OR ACTION OF forming new ideas, or images or concepts of external objects not present to the senses.— *Oxford Dictionary*

Throughout my life, I think I have reinvented myself more times than I can remember, each time creating a better version of myself.

Ever since I was a small child, I have had the gift to always want to be more than I currently was. From a young age, I have traveled looking for an opportunity in all walks of life to better myself. I never expected my circumstances to define me; my imagination has always been present and, looking back, the truth is what I thought, about I became. Every goal I have set for myself and every little creative idea I have achieved in some form or another is because of my active imagination. I believe this is why I am where I am today.

This book is one of my many goals and I am still growing, still expanding, still dreaming, but, most of all, I have the dominant attitude that anything is possible as long as I can believe and see myself doing it. It is evident to me that in order to accomplish or create, we must use imagination.

In order to believe in imagination and its power, all we need to do is look at some of the greatest minds of accomplishment that have lived.

Albert Einstein, Henry Ford, Nikola Tesla, Abraham Lincoln, da Vinci, Beethoven, Steve Jobs, Stephen Hawking, and the list can go on and on but the fact remains—they all had a vision, they all used and understood the power of imagination to get where they wanted to go. Their imagination was the key to their success. Of course, this was always backed by their power to believe in themselves. They used their natural-born gift. They could actually visualize themselves doing the things they wanted to do, before even doing it.

Imagination plus belief fueled by emotions will manifest into reality.—Harley Hanson

Part 1: Your Mental Picture

Imagination has been responsible for all of mankind's discoveries. People had to have imagined something before they set out to do it. If you take away imagination, you take away motion and, without motion, nothing moves forward and nothing can happen.

Imagination is the beginning of creation. You imagine what you desire, you will what you imagine, and at last, you create what you will.—George Bernard Shaw.

We have crossed the world's oceans in search of new lands. We have built magnificent structures for all to see; we have invented trains cars planes that enable us to travel. We have built rockets to reach space, and technology to view the stars. All of this started life in someone's imagination. It is the spark that ignites the flame. Nikola Tesla knew the importance of imagination. Without it, nothing would be possible. You need to have a clear vision of the thing you want, and you have to be able to see the end result in your mind's eye—the mental picture of your achievement.

It takes curiosity to find your call to adventure, it takes courage to venture into the unknown, and it takes imagination to create your path.—Nikola Tesla

Facts and ideas are dead in themselves and it is the imagination that gives life to them.—Nikola Tesla

When I look back on my own experiences, every song I have written, every TV show idea I have had, all started in my imagination and, through a strong belief to reach my goal, I have accomplished it every time. What I have learned throughout my life is that when setting myself a goal, I must believe it is possible. I must see myself already at the finish line with my goal achieved.

By constant habit, I put the power of my imagination to work, and this power is limitless as long as we understand how to use it. I am by no means an expert, but it has never let me down. It is the connection between the conscious and the subconscious. It just takes practice and commitment to build that bridge. So many of us seem to forget about the power of our imagination. In our younger days it was always present. We enjoyed playing in our own make-believe worlds. Our thoughts were of fantasy and magic but unfortunately, as the years go by, our focus changes. We slowly lose our ability to use imagination to create.

We are mainly distracted by our worries and problems. We focus on bills to pay, the events of the world, and the drama that surrounds us in our daily lives.

You already know about the power of suggestion and how that can keep your mind busy, which is why you lose sight of your own goals and dreams. Instead you focus on things that will not give you a better quality of life. Focus on the negative, and what do you get? That's right, more of the same! However, those who succeed in life seem to have the ability to focus on their imaginative powers and hold their focus on that which they desire to create. It seems to be constant that they have this never give up attitude, and do not allow any distractions to take over their main focus.

But as we become more self-aware, and by reading this book and monitoring your thoughts, my hope is that you will start to think about what you really want in life. We can all find time to step out of our busy lives and build an imaginary picture of who we want to be or what we want to achieve—the secret is, we need to keep that picture in our focus all the time. We need to build the faith that we are working toward our goal. We need to see ourselves already at the finish line. If we look at this summary, we can simply say that all amazing achievers throughout the history of the world recognized that if they were going to succeed, they must have imagination. Imagination is simply a form of a picture you hold in your mind. You have done this many times before. Remember when you learned to swim or play guitar? At first you must have just imagined yourself doing it.

My point is, we all have a future; right now, our past experiences have put us in a type of survival mode—we focus only on our daily problems or needs. Our attention has shifted because of this. We lack imagination about our own futures and dreams.

We get stuck in this type of mental routine. To put it bluntly, if we keep doing what we have always done, we will keep getting the same result.

But if we remember that our imagination is the tool that transforms our ideas into reality, it seems clear that we need to go back to the mental state of using the imagination.

To bring anything into your life, imagine that it's already there.—Richard Bach.

POINT OF INTEREST

A team of researchers at Harvard Medical School investigated the power of imagination. The experiment showed us that our imagination not only alters our abilities but also changes the brain as if we were performing the actual act. The researchers took three study groups:

Group one was placed in a room with a piano, and a teacher gave them lessons for 5 days.

Group 2 was put in a room with an identical piano but told to do nothing.

Group 3 was put in a room with an identical piano and told not to touch the piano, simply imagine practicing playing the piano.

The results were shocking. Group 3, who had never touched the piano, only imagined playing, could play almost as well as Group 1. More amazing was that their brains had undergone the same physical change in the areas that control the finger movements. This just goes to show that simply imagining doing the act has almost the same effect as actually doing it. Amazing, right? You already know about the power of belief. I dedicated the last chapter to it. Now imagine for a moment you have this desire or goal you want to achieve. Do not hope you will achieve it; believe you will succeed.

On top of this belief, now I want you to start to imagine that you already have succeeded. Get a clear picture in your mind of where you want to be and how you would feel if it was already done.

Now stay with me—this is important!

Not only do you believe and feel, but now you can actually see yourself doing it or achieving it. Do you have any idea how intensified the vibrations you are sending will be? Without going into scientific research on the subject, we can simply say a lot more than just the belief alone.

If you believe and can feel the emotions as if you have already achieved the thing you want, then what is stopping you?

Einstein once said, "The true sign of intelligence is not knowledge but imagination."

Part 2: Visualization with Emotion

We can all set ourselves goals, and goals are important, but if we can't see and feel the emotions of what that goal will give us then the goal by itself is pointless. You need to get from where you are now to where you want to be when the goal is achieved. So how can we see where we are going if we are not even there yet? We need to use our imagination; we need to use visualization.

Look at visualization as the amplifier to imagination—it makes things stronger and clearer. It is like turning up the power and frequency of your mind. It is just your mind working backward, visualization is basically forming the mental picture that you have already achieved your desire. You need to trick the subconscious mind that you are already living the life you have always wanted, down to the smallest details.

It could be a new house, a better job, or even better health—whatever it is, you need to hold the picture in your mind. A great example of visualization would be—think of yourself on a job interview. Everybody is smiling, sitting across the table from you; you see the sunlight shining in from the windows hitting the table in front of you; you can smell that new office smell; and you notice how beautiful the flowers to your left are. You see the boss reaching over the table to take your hand while saying congratulations, you got the job. He says, in a very ambitious voice, "We are all looking forward to working with you." The next day you're hanging your nameplate on the office door. You feel amazed, you feel a sense of great accomplishment, and you now know that better financial days are coming. One thing less to worry about.

You see, you are creating a mental picture now even by reading this.

The key is in all the details and how you feel when it is accomplished. The more details you can visualize, the better!

The law of attraction teaches us how important it is to visualize. It takes practice, but through the habit of thinking we can make those images very real.

It builds the road between fantasy and reality. Remember, your subconscious does not know what is real or imaginary. The subconscious is also the creator of our limitations in life.

Whatever your subconscious believes changes your beliefs and in turn your self-perspective. You will get the mind-set that you can do it.

You are rewriting your subconscious, and when this process has been done, you change your own vibration. Remember your vibrations attract the things you want or don't want in life. But visualizing alone will not increase positive vibrations; you need to feel it. Our emotions seem to be the driving force of everything we do. The strongest of them is love. Anything is possible when we have the emotions that are compared with love. Everything we have done until now that is positive is because of the love emotion.

We get married because of love,

We protect our children because of love,

We travel and create because we love to do it,

And all the above is in reverse when the emotion of love is not present.

Now know this—our emotions are the most powerful way to change our thought patterns or the hardwired programming we looked at earlier.

We love our new understanding of life.

We love creating the new person we are going to be.

We love the power of auto-suggestion.

The emotional part of our visualization plays a crucial role if we want to create or manifest that which we desire. This is a powerful force. We use our thoughts, then we need to use our imagination to see what we want, and we use our emotions to feel like we have already achieved it. This creates an unstoppable force that sends out the signals or vibrations to the universe. It is amazing how Buddha, in the fourth century CE has already tried to teach us this.

What you think you create, what you feel you attract what you imagine you become.—Buddha

So, the next time you're unhappy with your life or you would like to become a better person, start to visualize the life or the person you want to create. Feel how you would feel when you have created it but most of all, believe it is possible.

It is just habit force at work—the more you do it, the more you can accept it as real, the more real it feels, the higher the vibration force.

If we want to know the secrets of the universe, we should focus on the nonphysical aspects rather than physical ones, that will speed up the inventions." So that's it—the trio—energy, frequency, and vibrations—are all nonphysical aspects.—Nikola Tesla

Believe it, see it, and feel it = receive it!

CHAPTER 6

AWARENESS

BY NOW YOU ARE READY to understand awareness and what awareness levels really mean. If we can control what we are thinking and can be aware of our own patterns of thoughts, we can change our behaviors. When our behaviors change, we change the outcomes in our future!

When we understand what awareness really means we can also change our views toward others. When we become aware of our thoughts and the emotions that guide us, we gain control in the present moment, which shifts our vibration. Everything is energy and the way to control that energy is by awareness. When we start focusing on what we are thinking and why we think the way we do, we start to create a mental shift from the autopilot mode.

Every chapter you have read so far has been leading up to this. My hope is that your awareness is growing and you are reaching a new level of awareness. Nothing is real unless you put focus on it—sounds crazy but it is true.

A great example of this is what we are taught in schools—that back in the fourteenth century, people actually believed the earth was flat. It was only after the advancement in technology that we now know that the earth is not flat. But if you do your research, you will find that as early as the sixth century there is documented proof of the spherical earth concept, and it even appears in ancient Greek philosophy. There are even those today who believe the earth is flat. My point is, it does not matter! If you put focus on it and believe it to be true, then it is true to you. It is the same for all beliefs, whether it is success, religion, or health. I'm happy, I'm sad, your mind is your reality. If you, for example, took a random person off the street and told them that they are simply a vibration of energy connected to everything, and that the way they feel and act on a daily basis is all due to their subconscious programming, it is highly possible that the person in question would dismiss this information because it goes against their own beliefs. They would form a systematic opinion on you, they would probably think you are insane or on some kind of drugs. This simply shows that their level of awareness is different from your level of awareness.

Awareness allows us to get outside of our mind and observe it in action.—Dan Brule

In ancient civilizations, mankind feared the heavens. They had the belief that thunder was a sign from the gods that the gods were displeased with them. As the human mind has evolved over the centuries, so has our level of awareness. We now know that thunder is just rapid expansion of air around the lightning bolt that sends out vibrations of sound. But they believed it was the gods so it was true. Well, at least to them. You see, my point is, whatever you believe to be true is true for you, and only you can control that. It is the same for all beliefs. Some of the beliefs can benefit you and motivate you whereas other beliefs will hold you back. It is said that there are two sides of the scale—ignorance and knowledge, but these are after all only man-made words—they only represent our levels of awareness on certain subjects or our personal understanding and beliefs.

Knowledge simply means that an individual has dedicated their time to absorb information needed on particular subject. This raises their level of awareness.

So, what is ignorance? Ignorance is only a lower level of awareness. Ignorance is simply a lack of knowledge or awareness of the particular information. We can all learn new information if we are willing to expect it!

When the student is ready the teacher will appear. When the student is truly ready... The teacher will disappear.—Tao Te Ching.

All around you can see people with different levels of awareness. It does not make a person less or more. The information in this book changes your level of awareness if you choose to accept it. Not everybody is aware of the powers that control our possibilities to build a better future for ourselves or to be a happier, fuller person. You are a product of all the information passed down to you, and not all of that information was correct or useful to your future.

Everything so far has had some effect on you, but are you aware of this?

Do you truly know why you are the way you are?

Without awareness of your own level of awareness, nothing can change.

Let us look at some examples I'm sure you will see the pattern I'm getting at.

If you see somebody who is poor, they did not choose to be poor. However, they are not aware of how they can change their current status in life.

If you see or know of a person doing criminal acts to gain better financial status, it is simply because of their lack of awareness to change. They are not aware of what is possible in life if they put their minds to good use. They are simply making money the only way they know how.

If you observe a person with a bad attitude, it is because they do not have an awareness of how their thoughts and emotions have been programmed in the subconscious mind. They are simply running on autopilot mode. They have little understanding of how their attitude affects their own outcomes in life.

If you know somebody who is depressed all the time, they do not have the awareness of their own emotional cycle and how to correct it.

If you see somebody driving like a mad man, they have little or no awareness of the dangers they could cause others and themselves.

All these things cause us to have an emotional response or judgment toward others. However, when we understand the levels of awareness, we can start to look at things from a different perspective.

You can't say the person is stupid or good for nothing, it is simply their limited awareness of themselves and what is possible in life. Their past experiences, and what they have observed and been told is what has made them who they are. They neglect and lack the information to see and understand what is possible through the power of being aware of all the things I have written about so far . . . Hopefully, you can see where I'm going with this—if we don't look for knowledge and understanding, we will not find it.

When the student is ready the teacher will appear. When the student is truly ready . . . The teacher will Disappear. — Tao Te Ching

Knowledge can light the path but you must be ready to walk it—Harley Hanson

PART 1: SELF-AWARENESS

Self-awareness is conscious knowledge of one's own character and feelings.

We now understand how important it is for us to feel and think positive if we want to change our lives and, at the core, we see it is our thoughts that control our behavior. And I'll say it again—please remember, whatever you think and feel will affect your vibration.

Cognitive neuroscientists have conducted thousands of studies that show us that only 5 percent of our thoughts, emotions, actions, behavior, personality is from the conscious mind; the remaining 95 percent comes from the subconscious mind.

This only reinforces the fact that 95 percent of your thoughts and beliefs come from your default program. Your autopilot mode. We often lack the awareness and knowledge of our mind function as to why we act and feel the way we do. But now you know, so ask yourself what you are going to do with this information.

Will you walk the path? Will you start today to change everything?

What you think you feel, and how you feel affects the way you act in the present moment, and what you do in the present moment affects your future.

Can you see the cycle now? Sorry if I repeat myself, but I really want you to become aware of who you are and why you are you. AUTO-SUGGESTION.

In psychotherapy, there is a practice called Cognitive-Behavioral-Therapy in which we see the same type of cycle. It teaches us that our thoughts cause our feelings and our feelings cause our behaviors. So, if you want to change your mind-set, it seems logical that the main focus should be your thoughts. You need to become aware of what you are thinking in the present moment, RIGHT NOW. And I hope by now, when those negative thoughts pop up in your mind, you will know it is only because of your default program. You will be aware you need to change or rewrite this program.

But how do we change something that is so systematic?

Just like auto-suggestion, we need to pay attention to what we are feeling and why. A kind of self-analysis. By doing this, you are putting awareness into your conscious mind. You recognize your emotions and feelings, and understand how your thoughts impact your behavior. This is the definition of self-awareness, and only when you are aware can you start to improve your life.

We all have a million thoughts running through our minds all the time, and a lot of these thoughts are of a destructive nature. These thoughts or negative beliefs are what is holding us back from achieving and excelling in life.

When I personally came to understand this, I learned a few techniques from psychology books to help me on my way. Through my own awareness and desire to change I started to notice my negative thoughts, and every time one popped in, I would visualize a big red stop sign and I would say to myself STOP, I will only focus on positive, get out…. This type of negative thinking will not help me build a better future, SEE YOU!

And the crazy thing is, through the habit of self-awareness it actually works.

Trust me, I needed it. We all have our demons and nobody is perfect, but through the habit of thinking we can all improve into a more positive person. We can all work toward the person we want to be. The most important thing is that you are happy with yourself and you understand that anything is possible when we have the right frame of mind.

Question:

How do we avoid negative thoughts?

Answer:

Through your present moment awareness—a type of self-analysis!

Through this type of awareness, you have the power to shift the direction of your negative thoughts to more positive ones, and when this happens your energy and vibration changes.

Each one of your thoughts has its own vibration frequency of energy, and your vibration frequency will only change to what you put the focus on.

What we focus on, we send out to be received by the universal energy field.

Yes I'm repeating myself, and you know why.

PART 2: AWARENESS OF THE UNIVERSAL ENERGY FIELD

Universal energy field: if you are a religious person, you might call this god.

Others like to use the terms—the universal mind, the higher consciousness, the quantum field, source energy. Whatever walk of life you come from, and whatever term you choose, the meaning will be the same—it is "omnipresent."

Omnipresent simply means, the unknown power that is present all the time. As science has proven, everything in the universe is made up of unseen energy, and this unseen energy is all connected—the energy field. We know that all energy vibrates at its own frequencies, and we are made from the same energy, meaning we vibrate at a frequency. By the Law of Vibration, whatever vibrations your subconscious mind is sending out, your thoughts and feelings go out into the universal mind/universal energy field.

In turn, the universal mind will answer you, you get back more of the same vibrations of the same frequency you are sending out (Law of Attraction). Like attracts like, positive attracts positive, negative attracts negative.

This is by no means just a philosophical idea. It has been around throughout the ages, and is now a scientific fact. Understand it, believe it, and most of all, apply it in your daily life.

You are just like a magnet, whatever frequency you are sending, whether it is positive or negative, you are sending it out into the universe, the energy field. Just like a magnet, you attract back whatever you send out.

The people, the circumstances that come into our lives are always similar to our dominant thoughts. The field is the bridge that connects everything.

Think about this—the sun is responsible for all life on earth. It is constantly sending waves of cosmic energy to earth. You cannot see these waves, but you understand their power. Most people rely on their five senses to understand reality. There are things present that we cannot see, but that does not mean they are not there; we are just limited beings of awareness when it comes to the grander scale of things.

Energy is omnipresent, omnipotent, and omniscient.

Your thoughts are vibrational energy.

Vibration energy makes electrons.

Electrons are charged particles that make up the atom.

The atoms build molecules.

The molecules build organisms.

Organisms live on planets.

Planets are components of the universe.

The universes are components of galaxies.

The system is the same everything is energy.

You are energy living in an energy field.

If vibration can change under consciousness, the vibration of energy must be consciousness.—Harley Hanson

When you control your thoughts and feelings, you control your vibration!

Now you are aware.

CHAPTER 7

YOUR JOURNEY SO FAR

BEFORE WE MOVE ON TO the final chapter, I think it is important for you to realize how far you have come. Everything to this point has led you to an understanding about how you view yourself and the world around you.

My goal was to give you the foundations you needed to build upon. I sincerely hope that the information so far has helped you to understand and believe that inside you there is a great power and only you can summon this power to change your life.

Your potential as a free-thinking human being is endless. You are what you think you are, and your limitations in life are only what you believe them to be. Through the power of auto-suggestion and awareness you can learn the principles you will need to create a better life for yourself.

I told you at the beginning of this book that I don't consider myself as an amazing writer, but I do know the importance of habit and repetition. That is why, until now, the book has been structured the way it has. Before we move on to the next chapter, let's look at the journey so far and see what you remember—repetition is the key . . .

Here we will do a quick recap of the information so far. I would tell you to read the whole book again because I have learned that every time you read the same book, more information sinks into the subconscious mind. However, that is your choice. So, let us take a quick look.

CHAPTER ONE: UNDERSTANDING WHAT YOU ARE

Quantum Physics/Quantum Mechanics has shown again and again that there is no such thing as solid matter—it simply does not exist in the known universe. Everything in the universe is made of atoms, and advancements in scientific equipment and understanding shows us that everything on a subatomic level, when analyzed in its most basic form, consists only of invisible energy, and that energy is a vibration of frequency.

This means that everything in our reality, including ourselves, has no solid physical structure. It is all made up of the same energy.

And that energy is constantly vibrating. You are, therefore, a vibrating being off frequency.

YOU ARE A TRANSMITTER AND RECEIVER OF FREQUENCY

The human brain is both a transmitter and receiver of frequency. Your mind is like a radio tower sending out and receiving signals (Vibrations) all the time.

These frequencies are received by the universal mind or the universal energy field that connects everything.

What you send is what creates your circumstances in life. Some of the greatest minds in history, like Thomas Edison, Nikola Tesla, and said it best with their inspiring quotes:

Both Albert Einstein and Thomas Edison said—The human brain emits frequency which when focused, picked up by another human brain, and does affect physical matter. It passes through the ether, through solid objects, and travels faster than the speed of light. There is a magnetic pull.

CHAPTER TWO: THE LAW OF VIBRATION

The law of vibration is one of the basic laws of the universe. It shows us that everything moves, nothing rests, and our reality is literally an ocean of motion.

Once we come to understand that we are all vibrations of frequency and our thoughts and emotions amplify those vibrations, we can then start to see a small part of how the universe works.

The key point is, if you think negative you send out negative vibrations of frequency and you receive back whatever you are sending out.

All thought is a form of energy, a rate of vibration, but a thought of the Truth is the highest rate of vibration known and consequently destroys every form of error in exactly the same way that light destroys darkness; no form of error can exist when the "Truth" appears, so that your entire mental work consists in coming into an understanding of the Truth. This will enable you to overcome every form of lack, limitation or disease of any kind.—Charles F. Haanel

CHAPTER THREE: CONSCIOUS VS SUBCONSCIOUS

The human mind is a powerful piece of biological equipment. It is capable of so much. The mind is the great designer of both creation and destruction.

There are two basic areas of the human mind—the conscious and the subconscious.

The subconscious can process 40 million bits of data from the world around you every second. The front part of your brain is consciousness; it can process only 50 bits of data per second. This will show that the subconscious is 1 million times more powerful than the conscious mind.

CONSCIOUSNESS

Consciousness is your awareness of everything you have experienced so far. Without consciousness, we would not exist because, if we did exist, we would not know it.

THE SUBCONSCIOUS MIND

From day one of your life, the subconscious has been busy recording information, some of this through experiences and some of it from what has been given to you in the form of information, and your subconscious never sleeps. It is always at work.

It does not know what is right or wrong and, over time, the information that has been given to you becomes your default program. Your emotions and actions go into a kind of autopilot mode. Whatever the subconscious believes to be true is true. It is the subconscious that is responsible for your limitations in life or your lack of motivation in yourself.

The subconscious does not understand the difference between what is imagination and reality. This is important to remember when using visualization techniques.

SUGGESTION

A suggestion is a powerful thing. All your life is built up by suggestions. These suggestions have programmed the subconscious mind.

AUTO-SUGGESTION

Auto-suggestion is a way you can influence the subconscious mind—just like your computer, you have been running on the default program. Your personality, your attitude, your current status in life is all due to your default program. If the power of suggestion wrote this program, it seems only natural that the power of suggestion can rewrite the program. This is where auto-suggestion comes in.

By creating a new belief pattern and telling yourself, through habit, positive things, we can slowly rewrite this program.

CHAPTER FOUR: THE POWER OF BELIEF

Throughout our lives, we can see great evidence of how the power of belief works. We see it in all great human achievements and discoveries. We see it in the athlete, we can see it in the music industry, and it is always constant in the business world when related to success. Without belief, no achievement is possible. Belief is simply a frame of mind. It is the constant motivation to succeed. It is the ability of the mind to not accept failure and to push on, no matter the odds. It is what separates success from failure. Life isn't about finding yourself. Life is about creating yourself.—George Bernard Shaw

CHAPTER FIVE IMAGINATION

Imagination plus belief fueled my emotion = the manifestation into reality.—Harley Hanson

People had to have imagined something before they set out to do it.

If you take away imagination, you take away motion and without motion, nothing moves forward and nothing can happen.

We can simply say that all amazing achievers throughout the history of the world recognized that if they were going to succeed, they must have imagination.

VISUALIZATION

Visualization is the amplification to the imagination. It makes things stronger and clearer. It is like turning up the frequency of your mind.

It is like working backward. Visualization is basically forming the mental picture that you have already achieved your desire. You need to trick the mind that you are already living the life you have always wanted, down to the smallest details. It could be a new house, a better job, or even better health—whatever it is, you need to hold the picture in your mind. But visualizing alone will not increase positive vibrations; you need to feel it too. Our emotions seem to be the driving force of everything we do. The strongest of them is love. Anything is possible when we have the emotions that are compared with love. Everything we have done until now that is positive is because of the love emotion. The emotional part of our visualization plays a crucial role if we want to create or manifest that which we desire. This is a powerful force for our thoughts. We need to use our imagination to see what we want, and we use our emotions to feel like we have already achieved it. This creates an unstoppable force that sends out the signals or vibrations to the universe.

What you think you create, what you feel you attract what you imagine you become.—Buddha

CHAPTER SIX: AWARENESS

When we become aware of the emotions that guide us, we gain control over the present moment, which shifts our vibration.

Everything is energy, and the way to control that energy is by awareness.

Ninety-five percent of your thoughts come from your subconscious mind, and your thoughts affect your behavior and your personality.

So, if, for example, you have negative thoughts, this is all due to the program your subconscious is running on.

We often lack the awareness of why we act and feel the way we do. We just run on autopilot mode. If we want to break this autopilot mode or rewrite the hard drive, we need to pay attention to what we are feeling and why. A kind of self-analysis.

To put it bluntly, pay attention to why you feel and act the way you do, and change it to a more positive state of mind.

That state of mind creates your thoughts and emotions, which change your vibration frequency. Whatever frequency you send out into the universal energy field is what you will attract back. Like attracts like.

Ok, recap over.

By now if you have truly come to understand this information, you will understand that the teachings throughout time are all connected—they have all tried to teach us the same thing. And that the greatest power in life is the one you have inside of you. When you become aware of this and have faith in the information and what it all means, then you have the foundations to start changing your life for the better. Everything in history, every great accomplishment, every religious movement, every major scientific breakthrough—all started with a belief, and when that belief becomes the foundation and gets hardwired in the human mind, nothing can stand in its way. But you must believe in yourself! The evidence is out there—anyone can change, and anyone can achieve their desires if their frames of mind are right!

The past has gone. There is nothing you can do to change it. The only thing you can change is your perspective of your past.

In the present moment, don't let it control your future. The present moment is all you have—your current awareness and your attitude toward the future. Only by changing your thoughts and setting your goals and believing will you have the power to change everything.

Please ask yourself right now—What do I want in life?

Can I break the chain of old habits and start living to my full potential?

If you hear that inner voice saying yes, then turn over the page...

Once upon a time, the subconscious mind said to the conscious mind that there is a great storm coming; come back inside where it is safe; we must stick to what we know. We don't need to take chances in the storm! We don't need to change our routine. I am comfortable here... The conscious mind heard the subconscious, but this time it did not obey. The conscious mind had a secret weapon—AWARENESS. I will go through the storm, said the conscious mind, because on the other side there is a brighter day.

When you commit to change, then and only then will change happen.

If a guy with my history can do it, then I am 100 percent sure you can do it.

CHAPTER 8

WHAT HAPPENS NEXT CHANGES EVERYTHING

IN ORDER FOR THINGS TO change, you must really want change, not just an idea or wishful thinking. You must be ready and 100 percent focused on what you want. You must always be aware that there are a million and one distractions out there or a million excuses why you can't. If you look for excuses, you will find them. If you believe deep down inside that it's hopeless, then guess what—you are right, because what you believe to be true is true for you.

Look at it this way—your attitude toward yourself and your beliefs and limitations is simply your default program running! You have been programmed this way. You have been running on autopilot until now.

Remember, anybody who has achieved anything in life has done so simply because they did not get distracted. They did not let the power of suggestion steer them away from their desire, and they kept 100 percent focus on themselves until the goal was achieved. You don't need me to tell you this. The evidence can be found in every successful person. It is easy for us to look at someone who is a successful person and say, oh well, they were lucky. However, I am sure that behind that story of success there is a person who may have failed many times, but they simply refused to give up. They formulated a plan of action powered by their own belief until their success was a reality.

Success is not final, failure is not fatal: it is the courage to continue that counts.—Winston Churchill

From now on, keep your focus on yourself, and always remember that the only person that can better your circumstances and results in life is you!

No more excuses.

No more blaming circumstances or others.

You are in control of your future. It is designed by your own thoughts.

Wherever we look on this planet we call our home, we see people anxious for their circumstances in life to change. However, if you look a little deeper, you will also see that they are unwilling to change themselves. That's why nothing in their lives will ever change. They lack the inner understanding and power, and that power is realization! Combined with awareness! Realization of yourself, who and what you are, and awareness of how to change everything.

You need to be the person you need to be in order to get where you want to go. If not, your old self and habits of thought will continue to keep giving you the same results in life as you have been getting so far.

You can read 100 books on the subject, but if you don't put into actual practice what you have become aware of, your old habits and beliefs will just keep running in a kind of loop. That's right! You just keep running on autopilot. Look around you, how many people do you see taking control of their lives? I am pretty sure not many. Why?

Because they don't even know where to start. But my hope is, if you process this information and accept it, you will, soon.

The world as we have created it is a process of our thinking. It cannot be changed without changing our thinking.—Albert Einstein.

They say knowledge is power, so that being said, if you have knowledge of yourself that would justifiably mean self-empowerment. When it all comes down to it, we know we are all made of the same stuff—ENERGY.

Yet some of us are happy and others are sad, some of us are rich and others are poor. What is the science behind it? We know we all have had different experiences and impressions earlier in life, but there is one fact that remains—the only thing that separates us is our state of mind. If you want things in your life to change, you need to change things in your life; the only way to do this is from within.

So far, I have given you the information you need to have the strong foundations we talked about. It is now your choice, and yours alone, to decide—will you use this information to start to change everything? Will you build that skyscraper or simply let those new foundations crumble away? The choice is now yours.

If you accept the information so far, then you are ready to create a more positive version of yourself from the inside out. The idea is, when you have finished this book, you will be able to create the circumstances and opportunities in life you want. But this can happen only if you stay focused. When you are focused, anything is possible. From here on, it is critical that you understand that the information given to you in this book is based on your own inner power. It has always been there, just waiting for you to unlock it, and through this new awareness, it's yours to use.

Ask yourself, do you believe in you?

Are you ready to make change happen?

By now you will have come to understand that everything is connected by an invisible energy field, and this energy field is made up of frequencies and vibrations. Your thoughts project their own unique energy in the form of the same vibrations and frequencies. Whatever your state of mind is, your thinking patterns will all affect your vibration. This, in turn, will affect and attract your results in life. You have the knowledge needed. Now you need to become the master of your own mind and take control of your life.

So, let us look at how to do this. When you put attention on something, you become aware. And when you are aware in the present moment, things start to change.

Do not dwell in the past, do not dream of the future, concentrate the mind on the present moment.—Buddha

PART 1: SELF-ANALYSIS
From *Seat of the Soul*

By choosing your thoughts, and by selecting which emotional currents you will release and which you will reinforce, you determine the quality of your Light.

You determine the effects that you will have upon others and the nature of the experiences of your life.—Gary Zukav

Ok, let us put things into practice. I would like you to grab a pen and some paper in order to make notes as we go. Writing things down will help you focus on the present moment, and this is also something you can reflect on later. If you don't have a pen, just read through the chapter, but please come back and do the exercises. Commit yourself to change.

Before we start, the first step is to be completely honest with yourself. Why are you, you? Have you ever really thought about that? If, for example, you have negative thoughts on your own limitations, simply ask yourself—search your mind why you feel and think the way you do, where did this default program come from? Your default program has been running nonstop until now. This program is the way you feel and act automatically due to your subconscious mind. The crazy thing is, in life we never really stop and ask ourselves these types of questions. We are all always too busy or distracted.

By asking yourself questions, you start to put your own awareness into action.

This is a great exercise I personally do often when the mind is quiet. I focus on a particular question or problem, and sooner or later the answer presents itself to me. You will be surprised what memories you have; the answers you seek are all in there. Some people even believe that the subconscious can send out the question into the universal field, and it is the field that can give us the answers. Whatever you believe it to be, the results will be the same.

Your life—and everyone else in the Universe is playing the part that you have assigned to them. You can literally script any life that you desire, and the Universe will deliver to you the people, places, and events just as you decide them to be. For you, you are the creator of your own experience—you have only to decide it and allow it to be.— Esther Hicks, *Ask and It Is Given*

ARE YOU READY?

Now, on the top of the page, write MY BELIEFS.

Now be honest with yourself. Search your mind and don't hold back.

Write down all the things you would like to change about yourself—your thoughts, feelings, and actions.

Make a default thoughts list and a new awareness list. This way it's possible to see what you have learned. Simply by writing it down, you are putting your awareness into real time action.

Here is a basic example of what I mean. Right now, it is only hypothetical, but you will get the idea.

DEFAULT THOUGHTS

I get angry too easily.

I wish I had more patience with others.

I feel sad and sorry for myself because I had a bad childhood.

I'm always worried about money and my health.

I'm never lucky.

Now, once you have done this, use the information you have learned in this book to try to correct these thoughts. Here is my example.

NEW AWARENESS

I will use my own awareness to control my feelings in the present moment, to control my anger—I understand nothing good will come from my acting this way. And most of all, I want to send only positive vibrations out into the field.

I am now aware that not everybody thinks as I do. I will be patient and allow others to express themselves in the only way they know how to. And if I have nothing positive to say or add, I will shift my focus from the present situation.

My childhood was not my fault, and what has happened in the past was out of my control. However, I will not allow this to control my future. I am now in control from here on. The future is mine to create.

When I have fear and worry about money and my health, I will understand that this will change my vibration, only attracting more of the same. Through awareness I will only focus on the positive and believe good health and money flows to me.

My new mind-set is one of abundance.

OK!

You get the idea. Use what you have learned so far to correct your belief patterns. By writing it down, you are setting your mind to work. When you shift your focus from negative thoughts to positive through the habit of thinking, you start to rewrite your default program.

It's all about habit—the more you think positive, sooner or later the subconscious mind will accept this information and desired belief. The key is, the more powerful the emotion connected with the desire you want and the constant positive reinforcement, the faster the subconscious can absorb it.

Remember, all your limitations in life have been set by yourself, whether you are aware of it or not. It all comes from your previous experiences in life. Whatever you have observed or been told is what has been imprinted into your subconscious mind, creating your beliefs and limitations.

When you become consciously aware of something in the present moment, you have control. However, when your awareness shifts, the subconscious mind takes over.

Meaning, if you have your focus on your thoughts and emotions, the subconscious mind is not running them, YOU ARE!

But when you lose the ability of self-awareness in your present moment, your subconscious plays your default program—your old routines, thoughts, and beliefs.

Until you make the unconscious conscious, it will direct your life and you will call it fate.—C. G. Jung.

There is a story about the guardian angel that always follows you. When you say to yourself, "My life is awful," it writes down "Awful life." When you say, "My job is boring," it writes down "A boring job." And when you say, "My body is ugly,'" it writes down "An ugly body." And then it goes on and grants you all those wishes, because they are filled with strong emotions (sadness, disappointment, regret, self-loathing). That angel is your subconscious mind (original source unknown).

This is all basically negative self-talk built up by your own beliefs; you need to break this cycle, and you need to do it now.

One of the best ways to do this would to first be aware of what you tell yourself and, second, counter it with a positive thought.

For example, if your belief is, "I can't get a better or higher paying job because I'm not smart enough, I lack the skills needed," simply change that to "Now I'm ready and the right job and situation will present itself to me because I'm dedicated and strong-minded."

Remember, when you think positive, positive things happen. An opportunity or an idea will present itself. And when it does, you must act upon it.

Another great technique is simply using the stop sign I talked about earlier, or a delete button. Every time you notice a negative thought, simply say, stop, visualize that big red stop sign or your hand pressing the delete button. You have no time to focus on the negative anymore. Tell yourself, I am writing my own program from here on.

These simple practices simply show your awareness in the present moment and your new control. I know this is no easy task; it is like trying something new for the first time. It feels uncomfortable, and it goes against what you are used to but with a persistent habit and awareness, you have the power to control it and to change it. It's just like riding a bike for the first time. Sooner or later you will get the hang of it.

When you believe in yourself, anything is possible. These are not just words to inspire you. It's a fact. It all comes down to control and positive thinking and the habit of thinking and feeling positive.

No matter what, when you choose to be a better person and you have the emotions and beliefs of success, nothing will stand in your way!

Now you are starting to be aware, you do not use the term hope anymore.

Simply know it's true. BELIEVE.

PART 2: THE MASTER PLAN

In order to move forward or achieve something in life, you need a master plan. You need to know what you really want in life. Whatever it is you want to change, to do, or to have, you must set the final destination in your mind, and believe it is possible. But you must have faith—know that what you want wants you!

Look at your life like this—you are sitting in your car with no idea where you want to go! You will either sit there and go nowhere, or you will just drive around aimlessly and, before you know it, you will run out of gas—game over, life over.

Nothing can be achieved until you know where you want to go!

Every great success story, man or woman, they all had one thing in common—they all knew exactly where they wanted to go, and through their own beliefs and faith their goals were achieved.

One of the great resources of this information can be found in the book *Think and Grow Rich*, by Napoleon Hill. All of the 500 people he interviewed about the secrets of their success said they had a burning desire, and knew what they wanted! They had faith that they would achieve that burning desire, and it was their constant and main focus.

Now I need you to think hard really hard—what is it you want more than anything else? It could be something you want to achieve—a better job, or a new or improved relationship, or something creative, etc. It could also be something materialistic you want—like a new car, or a new house, a higher income—whatever it is, write it down on paper.

For this exercise, I want you to write, on the top of page, MY GOALS. Write down 10 things you want. For example,

1. I want a better job.
2. I want to travel more.
3. I want to be in better shape.
4. I want a new car.
5. I want to be financially independent.
6. I want to be in a relationship with my ideal partner.
7. And so on.

When you have finished the list, I want you to read through it. Try to see which five are the most important to you. Put a number between one and five to each of them, five being the highest desire and one being, I want it but it can wait.

1. Better job: 5
2. Want to travel more: 1

3. Want to be in better shape: 3

4. And so on.

Once you are down to five, do the same procedure until you get down to just one. It will not be easy, but at least this way you will see what it is that you really want. When you have finished, you will know what is most important for you in the present moment, and this is what you will focus on daily. You remember we talked about visualization? Well, here is where it comes into useful practice.

Once you have your major desire, close your eyes. Imagine yourself already in possession of, or achieving the thing you want. See yourself already there. Think how you would feel when it is done. Think about how your life would change. Hold that vision in your mind. Feel those emotions and how good you feel. Do this on a regular basis. Not only does it change your vibration, but it also helps with your motivation. Visualization is a great tool. It takes practice but it will really help you get into the state of mind you need to be in.

There are thousands of videos on YouTube to help with this. Just type in "how to visualize." When I did my list, I think I wrote the list close to 10 times but by the time I finished it, I knew my heart's desire. By identifying what you want, you set in motion a new thinking process. Writing your goals and desires down is a great way to manifest things into your life, and it works! I have used this technique constantly, and it works very well. I write my goal list in a journal and read it daily. On top of that, I write my goals down in places where I will see them often—like on my water bottle, on the bathroom mirror—the more I see it, the more it reminds me to hold my focus on what I want. The trick is to make sure your mind is visualizing as you're writing things down as well as when you see your reminders that you have hung up everywhere. You need to feel and act like you have already achieved your goal. You need to know that in your heart, everything is possible.

It is your subconscious mind that creates, and the subconscious mind speaks in pictures and thought (imagination, visualization).

When you repeat things, it embeds into your conscious mind as a thought. When that thought is constant, it goes into the subconscious mind as a belief.

This is basically the principle of auto-suggestion.

Once your subconscious mind holds that belief and your vibration changes, the law says that it must be the truth, and things will start to happen. Now you have a goal—you have set your destination. The Law of Attraction teaches us the same thing—that we need to keep our main goal in focus all the time. We need to use our imagination and visualize ourselves as if we have already achieved it. You need to act and feel as if you have already reached your goal or the thing you want to achieve.

Everything achieved by any mind is simply because they focused on what they wanted and, most of all, believed they could achieve it.

I AM THAT I AM (I am that I say I am, I can do what I believe I can do).

Success is the progressive realization of a worthy ideal.—Earl Nightingale

We must be the epitome, the embodiment of success. We must radiate success before it will come to us. We must first become mentally, from an attitude standpoint, the people we wish to become.—Earl Nightingale

PART 3: WHAT WE THINK IS OUR REALITY

If you read success stories or self-help books you have probably seen this saying a thousand times in many different ways: You become what you think about.

And whatever you believe becomes a self-fulfilling prophecy.

Philosophers have said it, the self-help books you read say it, gurus say it.

And now I'm saying it because it really works.

You become what you think. Or, as Earl Nightingale once said, "You become what you think about all the time."

A man's life is what his thoughts make of it.—Marcus Aurelius

If your own belief is that you are a failure, you will also find a reason to back this belief. You will view each failure as proof that you're not good enough. And if you succeed, you probably say, well I was lucky that time. Now I want you to understand that it is not your lack of skill or ability, it is only your beliefs that keep holding you back from achieving.

Positive beliefs and thoughts lead you on the road to better outcomes. When you think positive, you act positively. This will, of course, increase the positive outcome desired. Just because you think something, it does by no means make it true. Don't let negativity control your life.

When you believe 100 percent that you are successful and you do not entertain any other thoughts or self-doubts, then the magic happens—you simply become what you think about. When your focus is on you, the inner you, then real change starts to happen! If you don't believe me, try it yourself.

The greatest discovery of my generation is that human beings can alter their lives by altering their attitudes of mind.—William James

PART 4: THE LAST KEY

You, and only you, hold the keys to unlock the power of your mind. Simply by reading this book to the end you have set in motion a new understanding. My goal was to give you a greater understanding of what you are, and share with you what I have learned on my journey for knowledge so far. The reason I have repeated myself throughout this book is to help your mind digest the information presented. Like I said, the power of suggestion is a powerful thing when we know how to use it. By using the power of suggestion, combined with imagination, we can reach the subconscious mind to change our default settings and beliefs. I hope you have found inspiration and knowledge to change your life for the better from here on out.

The last key of information is to remember that the world around you is full of distractions; everything and anything can distract your way of thinking. Negative suggestions are present everywhere, and as long as you're aware of it in your present moment, you have control over this. You choose what you watch on TV, and what you read, or what you click on social media. Stay away from the negative things. You need to devote your thinking only to the positive from here on out. Whatever it is you want in life, hold that as your main focus.

This is something I decided to do a long time ago. I stopped watching TV and the news—in fact, the only time I watch TV now is with my children when we watch a family movie or something uplifting. The rest of my free time I use to read books or listen to inspirational speakers that will help benefit my life. I love just sitting in a quiet room asking myself questions and giving gratitude for how far I have come and what I have achieved so far. I try to look at all the great things around me in my life—like my children—and I am thankful for every day I'm alive. The point of all this is, I'm trying to take in only positive information and keep myself away, to the best of my abilities, anything that could change my thinking patterns. Another example is—when people around me talk negatively, I shift my focus. I do not engage in the conversation. I try my best to change the subject or reply with a positive comment. This one is still a work in progress. I must be aware of my old default program. Everything takes time but through habit, anything is possible.

These are just a few simple steps I have personally taken to help my mind-set and vibration. It has worked for me, and my results are undeniable. The universe is a mysterious place, but one thing is for sure—we are all made of the same energy, and our minds transmit and receive this energy.

Thank you for reading this book whoever you are. I know that if you believe in yourself, everything will change. So yes, What Happens Next Changes Everything.

On the next page, I will leave you with some recommendations for future reads. Keep a focused mind and keep the positivity up, and you will see great changes in your life.

Until next time.

Harley Hanson.

PS. One more time, just for the hell of it.

You exist in the field of energy, and everything is made of the same energy. This energy is a vibration of frequency. Your thoughts create their own vibrations, which are sent out into the universal energy field. Whatever you send out, whether it is positive or negative, you attract back the same kind of frequencies and vibrations, which materialize into your life.

YOU BECOME WHAT YOU BELIEVE AND THINK YOU ARE!

Get a clear picture of what you want!

Tell the universe it's yours.

Know—nothing can stop you when you believe and have faith.

Keep your vibration high constant and positive.

Work toward your goal with no distractions.

Show gratitude and understanding of life.

All you have is time. Use every second to your advantage. You can use the day worrying about the negative, or you can use it focusing on building a better here and now, which will change tomorrow.

I think you have got it by now. Repetition is the key. Now go back to the start and read it again, because every time you read it a little more information sinks into the subconscious mind.

Harley Hanson

RECOMMENDED READING MATERIAL

Information is the key to knowledge.

The Master Key System
By Charles F. Haanel

Power of Your Subconscious Mind
By Dr. Joseph Murphy

Think and Grow Rich
By Napoleon Hill

How to Raise Your Own Salary
By Napoleon Hill

E-Squared: Nine Do-It-Yourself Energy Experiments
By Pam Grout

As a Man Thinketh
By James Allen

The Secret
By Rhonda Byrne

The Divine Matrix
By Gregg Braden

The Magic of Believing
By Claude Bristol

Kybalion
By Three Initiates

The Biology of Belief: Unleashing the Power of Consciousness, Matter &
Miracles
By Bruce H. Lipton

You Become What You Think about: How Your Mind Creates the World
You Live in
By Vic Johnson

The Strangest Secret
By Earl Nightingale

WORDS OF WISDOM

Whatever you look for in life, you will find.
If you look for the negative you will find only more of the same.
If you look for the positive you will find more of the same.
Whatever you put your attention on you will be sure to find.

Some people are looking for miracles in life.
They neglect to see that there are 86,400 of them every day.
Every single second is a miracle when you show gratitude for life.
Nothing else matters.

Progress is made by motivation.
If you can't run, walk.
If you can't walk, crawl.
Whatever you do, just keep moving forward.

If you do things the easy way, life is hard.
When you do things the hard way, life becomes easy.
Nothing good comes by doing nothing.

There is no better time like now to decide what you want in life.
If you keep doing what you have always done, you will keep getting the same results.

If you can believe it and you can feel it,
You will achieve it.
It is a law.

95 percent fail because they give up on the first try.
Success comes to the 5 percent that never give up.

If you focus on the things you do not want,
You are simply attracting more of the same.

All you have is the present. Yesterday has gone and
tomorrow has not come to pass.
What you do think and feel in the present resonates into
tomorrow.

The greatest knowledge in life is to know oneself.
The greatest achievement in life is to control oneself.

You become what you think about most of the time.

You can be creative or destructive—the choice is initially yours.
All you need is awareness.

Life should never be a competition.
Avoid these thoughts.
Competition is for those that believe things are in short supply.

Life is abundant.

If you want to be rich, avoid thoughts of poverty or lack.

Your own vibration is the key!

They say knowledge is power, but the real power comes from within.

Harley Hanson was born in England in 1979, to working-class parents; spending most of his younger years in a small rural area in the East Midlands, England. He struggled academically due to dyslexia, and felt he did not fit in with any of the 'It crowds'. But he wanted more from life than what he believed his childhood environment could offer.

At the young age of 17, He left England to travel and worked in many countries. He met people from all social backgrounds and different cultures before finally settling in Norway in 2001

In Harley's own words, "I reinvented myself more times than I can remember, trying many different areas of work, it was a long hard road before I finally understood and found myself."

In 2008, Harley Hanson's life took a dramatic shift as he was diagnosed with heart failure—AV-block 3 and was fitted with a pacemaker to keep him alive. Since that day, Harley has reached for his dreams, producing music and TV shows with no previous experience. Just a drive to live his life to the fullest and let nothing slow him down or stand in his way.

Shortly after his first heart operation, Harley began studying child and behavioural psychology and to this day, he works in youth development for the Norwegian Child Welfare Services helping those in need.

In 2013, Harley began studying some of the great success philosophers like Napoleon Hill and Earl Nightingale. Understanding that the law of attraction was very real. However, Harley needed to go deeper and understand where the information originally came from and how it all really works.

By 2015, Harley digested information from many of the world's oldest religions and ancient texts, some of this information leading back over 7000 years.

Harley believes that using this information combined with the developments in quantum mechanics, we can start to see and understand how we are all connected and we all have the power to change lives for the better.

From dyslexia misfit to the academic author, the journey is yet not finished . . .

This book is dedicated to my two children, Melody and Phoenix. Whatever happens in life, may this knowledge teach you that anything is possible when you believe in yourself. -xx

Made in the USA
Columbia, SC
02 March 2021

33785060R00078